T0195861

A PATH TO EXCELLENCE

The Blueprint to Achieving Your Greatest Potential

TONY JETON SELIMI
(JETON TONY SELIMI)

BALBOA.PRESS

A DIVISION OF HAY HOUSE

Balboa Press books may be ordered through booksellers or by contacting:

Balboa Press
A Division of Hay House
1663 Liberty Drive
Bloomington, IN 47403
www.balboapress.com
844-682-1282

Because of the dynamic nature of the Internet, any web addresses or links contained in this book may have changed since publication and may no longer be valid. The views expressed in this work are solely those of the author and do not necessarily reflect the views of the publisher, and the publisher hereby disclaims any responsibility for them.

The author of this book does not dispense medical advice or prescribe the use of any technique as a form of treatment for physical, emotional, or medical problems without the advice of a physician, either directly or indirectly. The intent of the author is only to offer information of a general nature to help you in your quest for emotional and spiritual well-being. In the event you use any of the information in this book for yourself, which is your constitutional right, the author and the publisher assume no responsibility for your actions.

Any people depicted in stock imagery provided by Getty Images are models, and such images are being used for illustrative purposes only. Certain stock imagery © Getty Images.

Cover design by Colibrian (99designs.co.uk), Author Photo By Dianna Bonner.

Print information available on the last page.

ISBN: 979-8-7652-2955-2 (sc)
ISBN: 979-8-7652-2953-8 (hc)
ISBN: 979-8-7652-2954-5 (e)

Library of Congress Control Number: 2022910434

Balboa Press rev. date: 08/01/2022

Contents

Acknowledgements...ix
About the Author xv
Preface.. xxi

Chapter 1   Introducing Excellence...1
Chapter 2   It Takes Guts to Climb Greater Heights 10
Chapter 3   The Octagon of Excellence 25
Chapter 4   Adios, Mental Confusion: The Source of
             Avoidable Headaches 42

*Principle 1: To break free from ambiguity, clarify what
you want, why you want it, and when you want it.*

Chapter 5   Fine-Tune Your Vision of Excellence 51

*Principle 2: Awakening your astronomical vision
requires committing to something bigger than yourself.*

Chapter 6   Avoiding Challenges is Futile; Facing Them
             is Courageous 64

*Principle 3: To build your resilience, it is wise to immediately
confront any issues that arise and respond mindfully and objectively.*

Chapter 7   Stop When Something Does Not Feel Right
             or Look Right 72

*Principle 4: Making mistakes is human;
correcting them awakens your excellence.*

Chapter 8   Bridge the Gap between Your Current Life
              and Your Desired Life 79

*Principle 5: For better, more efficient, and
more effective results, seek expert advice.*

Chapter 9   Be in Sync with Evolution......................94

*Principle 6: To grow on the inside and
expand on the outside, collaborate.*

Chapter 10   What Goes Around Comes Around 102

*Principle 7: To unleash the power of gratitude,
graciously give and accept compliments.*

Chapter 11   Leverage the Power of Acknowledging Your
              Achievements.......................................111

*Principle 8: Continuously celebrating small
wins can change your physiology, strengthen
your psychology, and maximize your potential.*

Chapter 12   You Are Destined for Brilliance—Honor It..........122

Who Can Benefit from Using A Path to Excellence?.................135
What's Next? 137
A Path to Wisdom...145
#Loneliness: The Virus of the Modern Age.........................148
Fit for Purpose Leadership #3....................................151
The Unfakeable Code® 154
Take Off the Mask: Your Soul is Waiting..........................157
Living My Illusion: The Truth Hurts..............................160
Into Your Divinity: Climb Greater Heights 163
Mindfulness for Higher Productivity, Performance,
and Profits..168
TJS Evolutionary Meditation Solutions............................172
Vital Planning for Elevated Living...............................175

To you, the growth seeker, the change-maker, the student, the visionary entrepreneur, the business owner, the leader, and the dreamer who seeks answers to life's greatest mysteries and solutions to life's greatest adversities. To all of you who turn to self-mastery as a way to face head-on all of your challenges, fears, hardships, and nightmares that may otherwise cripple the development of your human potential.

To the curious aspiring athlete, musician, scientist, doctor, father, mother, son, daughter, and friend who is ready to face all that stops you from making your dreams happen with excellence leading the way. My loved ones, worldwide friends, teachers, clients, students, and fans seeking a way out of an undesired situation and wanting to learn empowering ways of thinking, living, and being. Those of you pursuing more imaginative ways to help you climb to greater heights, ensure your fulfillment in every step you take, and reach excellence in your chosen area. It is how you grow your influence, worth and service.

To the leaders, business owners, professionals, truth-seekers, educators, health, and other professionals searching for tools and solutions to consciously overcome the ever-growing personal, professional, business, and global problems.

To the excellence-hungry individuals who pursue to harmonize material and spiritual intelligence and awaken themselves to a life of unprecedented achievements, freedom, and fulfillment. To those ready to awaken dormant parts of your magnificent being, upgrade your psychology to recover pathways to excellence, and embrace universal truths and the wholeness existing in each of us. Through self-reflection, you'll find that all of you want to inspire decisive action and life-changing transformation in others, with excellence leading the way. Many people who wait to seek a way out of an unwanted situation may be angry, frustrated, and stuck. If this is you, you have decided to invest the energy, time, and resources needed to gain self-mastery and awaken those dormant parts of your being that can help you create extraordinary life experiences. It is how you will feel empowered, loved, and triumphant.

Lastly, to my family, my partner, Dr. Sc. Todorche Stamenov, and my spirit, who volunteered for this assignment and continues to guide me to its ongoing unfolding and fruition.

Acknowledgements

A book is always the result of all the experiences that simultaneously happen in our inner and outer reality. It would have been impossible to write this book without the love, support, and lifelong contribution from all the people who have been part of my life since the day I was born. It has been assembled from years of learning and unlearning, overcoming one challenge after another, and finding my calling, place, and role in the world.

The book embodies my lifelong quest for unraveling life's mysteries through continuous study and research into different life disciplines and philosophies. I acquired this knowledge by consulting thousands of business owners and people from all professional backgrounds that I now use to help people break through addictions, fears, phobias, health problems, relationship problems, mental health and identity crises, and leadership challenges. It also encompasses the knowledge I've gained through building a successful career in technology and leading and managing complex and large-scale multi-million-billion technology upgrade programs and software solutions. I feel blessed to have broadened my mental horizons from the books of thousands of authors I've studied, the writers of many of the blogs that I have read, the talks, workshops, retreats I have held, and the teachers' seminars I've attended.

We form unique relationships with people we date, get engaged to and marry, socialize with, learn from, and work with. Some touched my heart profoundly, and others challenged me to my core and turned my world upside down. For those who know me, I want to thank you for being the wind beneath my wings that helps me fly to higher grounds so that I can walk my path to excellence and fulfill my ever-evolving mission in life.

Your kindness, authenticity, and unconditional love helped heal my wounds, find my place in the world, and ensure my adventurous, freedom, and growth-seeking soul is never tamed. I would love to express gratitude to my partner, Dr. Sc. Todorche Stamenov, whose courage to leave behind all he once knew for love epitomizes what the road to achieving excellence is all about. Observing you overcome challenge after challenge, battling with your inner demons, and altruistically working during the COVID-19 global pandemic to save many lives inspired me to write this book. In seeing how selflessly you give your all for the one you love and to help others live, you've taught me, our families, our friends, and the nation the meaning of unconditional love. Thank you for all you do for others, for us, and for humanity. I love you for every moment we have shared, the good and the bad, and every argument and disagreement, dancing, smiling, dining, cooking, exercising, and traveling we've ever had. I am thankful for being a source of constructive criticism, immense inspiration, love, and wisdom.

To my late parents, Shaqir and Ljutvije Selimi, and my most avid supporters. There are not enough words to describe the caring, devotion, strength, patience, and unconditional love you've shown me and all of my siblings throughout our lives. Without the support and challenges you gave me, I would not be who I am today.

Mum, you taught me many life skills, you stood by my hospital bed when I was fighting for my life, and you instilled in me the importance of integrity, love, and speaking my truth. You created a healthy foundation in me of what love is and is not. You embedded the hierarchy of values that, to date, I embrace and continue to evolve on my journey to attaining personal excellence. Your life has been an inspiration to me and everyone who knew you.

Dad, you ensured that I spoke a few languages, had the best education one could wish for, and taught me treasured business and entrepreneurial skills that prepared me for overcoming every storm life throws at me as I journey into attaining the gifts of excellence. You both dedicated your life's work for my siblings and me to have an education and a better chance for a healthy, meaningful, and fulfilling life.

Although the civil war separated us physically for almost ten years, I am blessed to have always had a mental, spiritual, and heart connection that transcends time and space with you. I trust that my love, appreciation, and gratitude to you both for all the love you have given me is captured in this book, written with a heart calling to help others climb to greater heights and transcend to higher levels of awareness.

This book is my way of honoring and appreciating you both and our ancestors, families, friends, clients, teachers, colleagues, journalists, event organizers, global leaders, and readers. My long childhood dream of making a worldwide difference and pursuing a path to excellence against all odds led me to create unimaginable breakthroughs and put me on a mission to travel globally and teach others what I have learned so that more people can achieve their full potential.

This is my gift to every human being who has ever felt the icy touch of not being good enough, not having enough wealth, and not feeling worthy of reaching their fullest potential. This is a gift to those whose lives have been affected by the fear of being abandoned, judged, rejected, and unloved. I dedicate it to the thousands of people who have been part of my journey, particularly Elgerta Ismailaj, Anila Gremi Krushova, Nora Rodriguez, Tammy De Mirza, Dr. Pietro Emanuele Garbelli, Paul McMonagle, Yavuz Altun, Ibrahim, Janet Uribe, Maria Lopez, Sue Bannister, Bernard, Valentin Petreski, Maja Aceski, Nazim Rashidi, Rita Behadini, Fadil Çitaku, Qëndresa, and Neo Brahimi Nikolla, Zërijeta Jajaga, and the global businesses, individuals, and VIP clients I have had the pleasure of assisting through my integrated coaching and mentoring business.

I have been blessed to learn, be supported, and be challenged by extraordinary people. A big thank you to Joe Dispenza, Tony Robbins, Oprah Winfrey, Bill Gates, Steve Harrison, Daniel and Andrew Priestley, Mindy Gibbins-Klein, Deepak Chopra, Brian Tracey, Jack Canfield, Gary Vaynerchuk, Lewis Howes, Dr. John Demartini, and the many other excellent teachers, leaders, and change-makers. Your determination, callings, and vision in life have been paramount for me to continue my quest for excellence, discover life's truth, and teach what I learn to help others climb to greater heights. Your lessons have significantly confirmed that I am on the right track, leading others by being authentic, objective, and mindful. They can expand their human potential and excel in all life endeavors. I thank you, and I love you.

Thank you to the hundreds of people who have interviewed me on their TV and radio, shows and podcasts and to every person who has written about me in their blogs, magazines, and newspapers. Thank you all for your time, for what you do, and for the unwavering support to help me keep my promise to educate, inspire, and transform your audience's perceptions so they are encouraged to function at their best. Every conversation and interview has planted a seed and ignited an idea in your viewers', listeners', and readers' heads. It has brought inspiration, saved lives, and given hope to billions of people from all walks of life to reach excellence and be all they can be.

My thanks go to the millions of readers of my multi-award-winning and multiple-times best-selling books: *A Path to Wisdom, #Loneliness, Fit for Purpose Leadership #3, The Unfakeable Code®, and Novum #10.* Thank you for taking the time to share your heart-wrenching stories with me, the breakthroughs each of the books helped you create, and the Amazon reviews that inspired positive action in others.

Thank you to all people worldwide who have supported and challenged me in this journey to bring and share the message of hope, inspiration, love, and transformation. To John Corcoran of the John Corcoran Foundation and Nick Nanton, Esquire, of DNAFilms for the opportunity to be an executive producer in the new eye-opening documentary, *The Truth About Reading: The Invisible Crisis Hiding In Plain Sight*.

This book would not have been possible without my reviewers, my publisher, and the entire team of book experts and their capability and support that transformed my manuscript. They turned it into a life, a business, and a wise-to-have personal, professional, and business excellence guide for millions of people worldwide.

Thanks are also due to many of my clients for offering their stories, recollections, and testimonials and providing expert commentary and insights. Most of the people mentioned in my book have wholeheartedly shared their personal stories and have permitted me to use their names. I have deliberately changed or withheld the names of a few celebrity VIP clients to safeguard their privacy. Please accept my appreciation anonymously.

This book would not have been possible without the many months spent in lockdown, working long hours, and the commitment and consistency. It took sleepless nights, sacrifices, and discipline for my mind, body, soul, and heart to work in synchronicity so that this book could come to fruition. Thank you, and I love you.

Finally, may the rippling effect of *A Path to Excellence* and *The Octagon of Excellence* and its eight transformational principles help people achieve their potential and climb to greater heights. May this information be passed from generation to generation so, as a species, we can support each other on our journey to grow into our fullest potential and safeguard the sanctity of human life as we venture into space and make new waves.

About the Author

Tony Jeton Selimi was born on December 12, 1969, in Gostivar, Northern Macedonia. From an early age, his mother ensured he wore leg braces to correct a congenital disability. At the age of five, unbeknownst to his parents, he was sexually abused, and at nine, he was stricken by an illness that left him hospitalized. He fought for his life for almost two years.

If that was not enough, when he started high school in Skopje, he was bullied, threatened, and persistently told he would never achieve anything in life. Despite all the hardships, his academic prowess paved the way for him to graduate high school with the highest marks and be accepted to study at one of the top engineering universities in Zagreb, Croatia. Having finished his first year at university, at the age of nineteen, against his free will, he was conscripted into the former Yugoslav army to fight a civil war he, deep down in his soul, despised.

As the war continued to spread across other parts of former Yugoslavia, his life was miraculously saved by his commander, Grbovič Luka, who saw the deceit in the Yugoslav army and government. With the help of his late mother, who followed her motherly instinct and borrowed money to buy him a one-way flight to London, he found himself homeless, hopeless, and worthless.

These early challenges set the scene for a remarkable transformation during his late teens, twenties, and the rest of his life. Tony used all that pained him to catalyze a profound change by awakening an inspired vision to use all he learned to help others overcome the obstacles that falsely stop people from accomplishing their wildest dreams. His calling for traveling the world to positively impact people's lives and achieve more extraordinary professional, business, and leadership success kept him focused on his ongoing journey to educate, grow, and transform himself to achieve greater levels of excellence. His lifelong determination to climb greater heights was inspired by many of his life predicaments, especially during his army days when he lost family, friends, the country, and the identity he once knew. He experienced things no teenager ever should. When you believe you are unworthy of being someone and then discover that you are, it awakens an insatiable appetite for growth, knowledge, wisdom, and service.

Having worked many jobs to put a roof over his head, support his family in a war zone, and pay for his education, in 1998, Selimi ended up graduating from one of the top universities in the UK, University College London (UCL). He led and managed multibillion-pound technology-transformation programs in the private and public sectors for more than eleven years. In 2009, after facing another life-transforming crisis, redundancy, he decided to start his own business and pursue his heart's calling: to travel the world and teach others how to find the answers and solutions to life's obstacles and cope better with their daily business, leadership and personal demands and pressures.

Like a phoenix rising from the ashes, he went from being homeless and impoverished to successfully climbing the corporate ladder and becoming an internationally recognized leader in personal development. He is a professional speaker, an award-winning author, a filmmaker, a millionaire's life strategist, and a business coach specializing in human behavior, authentic leadership, and the psychology of peak performance, wealth, and success.

Tony specializes in assisting people in breaking through addictions, low self-confidence, depression, fears, self-deception, procrastination, phobias, mental imprisonment, and limiting beliefs to awaken their inner leader, maximize their human potential, and accomplish higher levels of achievement, growth, and fulfillment. He is known for his ability to see through people's problems, behaviors, language, thought patterns, values, unspoken communication, and disempowering beliefs. He uses these to help them rid themselves of the lies that conceal their authentic individual, which is loving, powerful, and worthy.

Working in the corporate world, overcoming many personal and professional challenges, and coaching people from all walks of life gives him unique insight into the magnitude of his clients' pressures, challenges, and callings. After all, it includes Fortune 500 CEOs, business owners, authors, entrepreneurs, managers, consultants, salespeople, scientists, doctors, royalty, music, film and TV stars, and politicians.

Senior executives of Microsoft, Apple, Facebook, SAP, Bank of America, Ignis Asset Management, Deutsche Bank, Ernst & Young, Santander, HSBC, and Mishcon de Reya across EMEA, Asia, and the United States seek his help to address personal challenges, improve their business performance, grow their leaders, engage employees, and increase team performance, productivity, and profitability. He creates customized training, coaching, and consulting strategies to help businesses improve productivity, performance, and profit and implement change programs, mental health, diversity and inclusion, and well-being strategies.

Through proven processes, Tony helps people build the confidence, firm foundation, mindset, emotional resilience, strategies, and plans to create truly unique and lasting spiritual and material transformations.

Tony is a qualified coach recognized by several reputable institutions, including the International Coaching Federation (ICF), the Institution of Leadership and Management (ILM), the Demartini Institute, the Complementary Therapists Association, and Martin Brofman's Foundation of Advanced Healers. He is also a certified Reiki Master Teacher.

As the beloved author of A Path to Wisdom, #Loneliness, Fit for Purpose Leadership #3, The Unfakeable Code®, Novum#10, and A Path to Excellence, he crafted the Octagon of Excellence Method, Behavioral Change Principles (BCP), The Unfakeable Code® Method, and the TJSeMethod: ALARM® as one-of-a-kind, modernized formulas for self-mastery, business growth, and building wealth, excellence, and fulfillment. It has been hailed as the new self-improvement tool, and it contains the most potent principles for maximizing business, leadership, professional, and personal potential.

His self-mastery authenticity, integrity, values-based methods, principles, and strategies create the psychology and the mindset people need to make the life outcomes they intuitively know they deserve and want.

Tony travels the world to educate and inspire people with enlightening perspectives, humorous metaphors, client success stories, and a heart-illuminating personal transformation journey. He provides answers to questions and gives practical solutions to life's challenges through his one-on-one consultations, talks, workshops, corporate training, mastermind groups, Vital Planning for Elevated Living custom-made business, and self-mastery advanced learning experience. He also writes inspirational articles for newspapers and magazines. He is a regular contributor to diverse media outlets, high-profile blogs, TV programs, podcasts, YouTube videos, books (print, digital, and audio), the Unfakeability Index Test, the Life Fulfilment Oasis app, social media, masterclasses, webinars, Udemy courses, and TJS Evolutionary Meditation Solutions.

He has spoken on grandiose stages such as the United Nations, Rotary International, the Cranfield School of Management, European University of Tirana, international film festivals, leadership conferences, the PSA, and the London Business Show. His TEDx talk, "Technological Armageddon: A Wake-Up Call," has been watched by millions of people and addresses the present and future challenges we will face and the opportunities we will create in the next hundred to thousand years with the rise of artificial intelligence.

His work includes films and documentaries like the Emmy and multi-award-winning The Truth about Reading and Living My Illusion on Amazon Prime and Into Your Divinity: Climb Greater Heights. This documentary series raises awareness of various life predicaments no human being can escape. Tony has appeared on more than eight hundred podcasts and radio and TV stations across the world, including interviews by Royal Correspondent Ian Pelham-Turner, Besim Dina on Oxygen TV, Top Channel Albania, by Jack Canfield and Brian Tracy in America, and on BBC, SKY, ABC, NBC, CBS, and FOX, reaching more than one hundred million viewers, listeners, and readers worldwide.

Tony founded TJS Cognition Ltd. with a heavenly vision to infiltrate his one-of-a-kind methods, principles, and teaching in business, leadership, government, education, and health care. In doing so, he aspires to inspire decisive action in the lives of billions of people, contribute to accomplishing the UN's seventeen sustainable development goals, and evolve human consciousness.

He promotes the importance of listening to your heart's voice, having integrity, and living daily according to your authentic values in your personal, professional, and business life. Excellence in leadership, entrepreneurship, self-mastery and spiritual development can make a huge difference in shaping our modern world. They play a vital role in our well-being, the future of work, health care, education, environment, economics, and governance. Tony loves researching and teaching topics that bridge spirituality, science, business, building wealth, psychology, energy healing, well-being, time, space, miracles, and belief.

As a world ambassador of excellence, equality, and empowerment and a positive role model, he uses his hard-earned fame and influence to promote the importance of authenticity, coaching, education, integrity, mindfulness, diversity and inclusion, equality, and purpose in our personal and professional lives and our communities, families, societies, countries, and the universe.

Tony's global work and a mission to positively impact one billion people's lives were recognized by the London SME Awards, which selected him as the winner of "The Most Visionary Entrepreneur 2020" and a "global educator to watch." He also won the Corporate Coaching and Recruitment Business Coach of the Year 2021 Award, Silver Winner of Literary Book Award 2021, and the Maincrest Media Book Award 2021 for A Path to Wisdom, #Loneliness, and The Unfakeable Code®. His book The Unfakeable Code® is also the Winner of the Titan Silver and Book Excellence Award 2022 ® in the Category: Personal Growth and Development.

No matter who you are or where you are from, this is your time to access your Inner knowing, plan, and transform your reality. Tony is known for helping people create the transformational business, professional and personal breakthroughs, leaving them with a sense of inner peace and feeling confident, elevated, inspired, and worthy.

To connect, follow, and obtain further information on what Tony can do for you, your family, your audience, your business, your country, and your leaders, teams, and organizations, please visit https://tonyselimi.com and https://tonyjselimi.com.

Preface

Far too many people never grow into their true potential. Not knowing how to overcome the challenges life presents can leave many discouraged, disengaged, and delusional. Instead of being inspired to overcome what crashes us, we succumb to temporary difficulties, pain, and stress that make us feel anxious, confused, disengaged, out of control, powerless, stuck, and unproductive at home and work. This is a growing problem in an uncertain world that is leaving behind a cosmic trail of mental, emotional, and physical health problems, as well as a significant rise in mental health issues, divorce, unemployment, and socioeconomic disparities.

I have been down enough, but something within me made me stand up and take the next step each time. When I felt like quitting, I remembered the pain I have been through and what I have overcome, and I continued building a stronger me and a more significant why. So, no matter what struggle you may be facing, remember to make yourself stronger and your why bigger. You can choose to change or remain where you are. You can choose to be a lion or a sheep. You can even make your pain evaporate so your purpose can fly. Whatever you choose is what you become. So, since a choice is yours to make, you may as well decide to be the most advanced, inspiring, and wise person so that others crave your vibes.

This awareness of our power inspired me to create original work that uses a combination of lessons from real-life experiences and scientifically proven self-awareness, self-growth, and self-mastery principles to find sustainable solutions to life's greatest adversities and challenges. I am inspired when I think of the billions of you who can use my work as a reason to believe in your dreams even when times are not in your favor. I have shared the most amazing formulae of success in this book to help you feel more confident, empowered, and accomplished while working on your aspirations, goals, and dreams.

Most of the content in this book is based on synthesizing personal, professional, business, and client breakthrough experiences and thirty years of research, lessons, study, and transformations. I have also shared the pains and the pleasures I've encountered living an adventurous, challenging, and combination of an equally painful and purpose-driven life. It focuses on how you can use the lessons from your struggles, hard work, and breakthroughs to build immense drive, clarity, energy, focus, and momentum. Every principle shared will make your journey to achieving excellence more achievable, bearable, and meaningful.

I believe that we wake up as new people every day because we never stop learning. When it comes to learning, the sky is the limit. Why? Because you are born divine, and it is your birthright to express the divinity of your infinity. Unfortunately, your life experiences coupled with the conditioning from the environment you live in may have conditioned you to think you are not.

I will share a simple eight-step process and scientifically proven principles you can easily follow to learn from your challenges and mistakes and never give up, regardless of the obstacles that come your way. As you read this book, indulge yourself in the much-needed transformation you have dreamed about for years. I will help you out as you take baby steps toward tackling any challenge and attaining excellence in your chosen area of life.

This book aims to address the things in your mind that make you feel frustrated, not good enough, lost, or stuck in life. It will awaken the desire to regain a sense of clarity, vision, and purpose. Yes, it's natural to feel demotivated at times, but the real winner is someone who knows how to rise back from their lowest ebb. Imagine if you knew for sure that you came to this world to carry out a unique role that nobody else can. Wouldn't you invest the energy, the money, and the time to dig out that purpose and take actionable steps that help you align yourself with it? How about consciously choosing to adopt an attitude of living each day like it's your last. My life's work and many of my client stories highlight those examples and lessons that shed light on the beauty of being resilient, persistent, and committed to your divinity and the goals you need to accomplish to get there—no matter how hard the situation gets.

I aim to educate, motivate, and inspire you, the reader, especially youths, to believe in the beauty of your dreams, even if you perceive that nobody is there to help you out. To enjoy the peace and comfort that growing into your potential gives you, it is sensible to learn to fight the wars life presents. While relying on others may be helpful temporarily, it is wise to learn to depend on yourself in the long run. Just take the journey yourself, get up each time you fall, and keep moving forward. As long as you keep learning from your mistakes, it does not matter how many times you fall and fail.

Lastly, I intend this book to be a source of immense hope and enthusiasm for you, the reader, to empower the eight key areas of life and become the best version of yourselves. May it bring you the gift of clarity and objective thinking and assist you in building a step-by-step plan that makes your spiritual, mental, emotional, physical, relationship, career/business, wealth, and social quests come true.

This is your chance to awaken and own your God-given abilities, look deeper into perceived weaknesses and strengths, and gain control of your attitudes, feelings, and thoughts. In learning to upgrade your mind's software, your psychology, you build the confidence to make a successful personal, professional, and business life. I wish you all the best in using the Octagon of Excellence principles that you will be learning more about throughout this book to create the sustainable happiness, purpose, and growth that your body, mind, heart, and soul have ever hoped for. Someday, you will be so proud that you did not give up. Let each trial life presents you with be a new reason to believe in yourself. It is what will help you keep falling more and more in love with yourself each day.

1

INTRODUCING EXCELLENCE

From the moment you are born, your destiny awaits you; it's yours for the taking. The opportunity to be an inspiring person exists as long as you do, and the only thing that can stop you from achieving it is yourself. Growing into your greatest potential and achieving excellence are often thought of as unattainable or impractical. Often, you are so bogged down by your consistent habits and routines that they become the norm for your day-to-day life. In fact, doing something "out of the ordinary" becomes nothing short of a test. In doing so, you confine yourself and restrict your full potential without even getting anywhere close to it.

Many of you, either conditioned by society or otherwise, believe that your life corresponds to the same actions. Get an education, get a skill, get a job, get a mortgage, get married, have children, work for two-thirds of your life, get a pension, and retire—and that's it. Yet, time and time again, there have been many individuals who have broken this norm and reached greatness—true pioneers of their respective fields—who started from where you are. You are destined for excellence. Reading this right now, in the initial stages of this book, might sound rather far-fetched, but when you finish reading this book, remember to revisit this very segment to remind yourself that you are destined for excellence—and you *can* achieve it.

You will cultivate this feeling throughout the course of this book. It will be something you will take with you on your journey in life. This innate desire to grow into our most significant potential is present in us all, but life bogs us down. Be it work, school, personal life, or otherwise, we all have multiple responsibilities to cater to. In the process of doing so, we lose sight of this innate greatness and diverge from this path. Many people give up on this journey because they:

- did not know what they truly wanted
- were told they couldn't
- felt powerless, stupid, or unworthy
- feared and didn't believe they could
- had no way of knowing how to do it
- couldn't dedicate themselves to it
- kept making and giving in to excuses
- did not have clarity, plan, and vision

Now, after more than thirty years of studying, bridging together science, psychology, technology, and universal laws, and assisting thousands of clients, I have deduced the perfect method to guide people onto the path of excellence in their chosen areas of life. Let us commence our journey and dive straight into just why you are destined for excellence.

Achieving the Impossible Becomes Possible When You Have a Big Why

Whenever we consider any successful individual, an often-forgotten fact of life is that we put them on a pedestal. Since they've achieved global recognition and accolades, we assume they are a step beyond us. However, this is far from the truth. Nearly all of the notable, successful entities in the world who have significantly contributed to humanity as a whole arose from relatively humble beginnings. Many of those individuals have changed the world's shape and nature as we know it today.

If the Wright brothers weren't as tenacious and resilient when it came to their first aircraft, we might have never taken to the skies. In fact, the very aircraft-control system they devised for their airplane more than a century ago is still used in aircraft today. (It's been modified to meet modern-day demands, but the same fundamental idea still persists.) Two brothers who didn't even have high school diplomas set the foundation of modern-day aviation! Imagine that!

Similarly, if it weren't for Bill Gates, a college dropout, developing the operating system that is now used by more than a billion people worldwide—solely based on a big why and a goal he set—I would probably be using a typewriter to write this book! The Wright brothers, Nicola Tesla, Sir Winston Leonard Spencer Churchill, Nelson Mandela, Bill Gates, Oprah Winfrey, Barack Obama, Usain Bolt, Elon Musk, Richard Branson, Madonna, Adele, Rita Ora, Dua Lipa, Simon Cowell, Steve Jobs, Jeff Bezos, and other people who have changed the world did so because they lived with certain principles and had clear-cut visions and goals that were driven by a big why and aspirations that they had planned to the dot.

Being raised in average circumstances does not restrict you from achieving above average results. I am living proof that anything you set your mind to is achievable. As a child, I was subjected to various forms of abuse. As a teenager, I was bullied, was forced to fight in a civil war I despised, and became a homeless refugee on the streets of London. As an adult, I faced anxiety, depression, discrimination, an identity crisis, loneliness, poverty, and inequalities that crippled my being. To make matters worse, I had to face people who got high by making others feel small with their homophobic and xenophobic comments. Little did I know back then that every adversity I faced would eventually help me clarify who I am, why I do what I do, and what do I want to dedicate my life to. This is important, yet very often underestimated, step on the journey to growing into your fullest potential.

Today, my why is to use all I have learned and continue to learn to change positively, impact, and transform the lives of billions of people. I've used the same principles of personal excellence you are about to discover and learn to overcome various life struggles and unforeseen roadblocks. Each one of them assisted me and those I have coached over the years to transcend disempowering mental concepts and align actions, behaviors, and plans with our big why. It is why I travel globally to coach and assist countless entrepreneurs, CEOs, businesses, celebrities, and people from all professions to create the personal, relationship, financial, professional, and business breakthroughs and results they seek. Most of them achieved their success because they did eight things:

1. They somehow managed to turn their pain into a purposeful vision that inspires them.
2. They envisioned their success and worked day and night to achieve it.
3. They worked with a set of priority of values and principles that were aligned with their astronomical vision, which was driven by a big why.
4. They established systematic plans to achieve their success.
5. They invested in working consistently with a coach who would help them overcome challenges, expand their vision, clarify the next steps, and keep them accountable and focused.
6. They never made excuses or blame others when things went wrong.

7. They saw anything that was not working as an opportunity to grow, learn, and transform and not as an insurmountable hurdle.

8. They didn't play it safe, and they operated from a place of willingness to fail; if they didn't, they would never create the ability to win.

Begin to do these eight things daily and willingly, and you may soon see things change for the better in your personal, professional, and business life. Doing what others refuse to do can give you the edge you need to find the success you want.

You may be afraid to fail because you're overly concerned with the judgments of others. You do the minimum and try to fly under the radar, but what would change in your life if you never were afraid of failure? If you want to bring your goals to life, an attitude that behind every mistake is an opportunity to learn will serve you well.

Unsuccessful people spend a lot of energy and time making excuses and blaming government, the economy, the customer, prices, or competition. Even if the excuses are all true, complaining about it likely won't improve the outcome, and successful people know this. No matter how justified you are, try never to make an excuse for any result.

Truth be told, many of us are not prepared for life's greatest adversity or are equipped with the knowledge from an early age of how each life challenge, fear, or pain can be a brilliant catalyst for reaching excellence. If we don't have an end in mind, how on earth will we know when we have arrived where we want to be? Suppose you are not living in harmony with a set of personal excellence principles to get you the health, the relationship, the family, the job, the career, the wealth, the customer, or the desired lifestyle you want. In that case, you will remain stuck in old paradigms designed to keep you imprisoned in the illusion created by disempowered expectations of you. If this is not what you want, it's time for you to embrace the importance of creating a clear life-fulfillment plan.

A lack of planning for the spiritual, physical, mental, emotional, relationship, financial, career/business, and social growth you want creates havoc and discord in your life. You don't plan a vacation without some sort of plan; why would you do the same for your life? Lack of precise planning, not knowing how to break through fears, self-imposed limits, overcoming challenges that cause us pain, losing hope, not seeking help, not choosing to live by priorities of actions driven by a hierarchy of authentic values, and giving up are the eight fundamental causes of failure.

Don't be fooled. Challenges do not end, and they do not get easier. However, you can get stronger, smarter, and soulful enough to face them head-on. You can utilize the challenges you face as stepping-stones to achieve greatness. Planning, using a set of principles for personal excellence, and facing adversities are going to be things you look forward to.

The Comfort Zone: Quicksand

To achieve greatness, fulfillment, and our true potential requires bravely venturing into uncharted avenues of life: the terra incognita. Throughout history, those who have made a significant difference for society's betterment have done so by completely altering and reshaping the existing conceptions that prevailed at the given time.

For many people, escaping the comfort zone deems to be the most challenging hurdle to overcome. Responsibilities bind most people, and they simply cannot take the risk to venture out of their comfort zones. They believe that trying out or even considering new avenues could result in something detrimental. These people often fail to recognize the endless possibilities that can be found right outside the comfort zone! Their lives are reflections of what's going on in their minds.

It's best to jot down whatever restraints you have when it comes to leaving your comfort zone. Much like the heading suggests, it is quite like quicksand. The more you convolute yourself in self-doubt and continuously question yourself, the deeper you will sink. The most effective way to break free is to use a streamlined method to pull yourself out. To break free of your comfort zone requires you to create a huge why to make you comfortable with discomfort.

The further you venture from the safety nets you have put up, the more you will discover. Ultimately, things you would once consider out of your comfort zone will become a fundamental part of it! In this pursuit of excellence, you need to remember that the journey begins with the very first step you take to clarify your authentic values and bravely journey outside of your comfort zone.

Why This Book?

Once you've read this far, you may be wondering what you will gain from this book. I have encapsulated my decades of teachings into an easy-to-follow method, and it will be a one-stop guide for excellence in your chosen area of life with a set of principles for any troubles you are facing in your life. You will walk away with a blueprint for achieving your greatest potential.

Everyday life became stagnant due to the COVID-19 global pandemic. At some point, most of the world's population had enough, some lost their jobs, and others struggled to cope with the loss of loved ones or making ends meet. For many people, years of hard work seemingly came to a halt. If that was not enough, the world watched in horror as Russia invaded Ukraine, creating another worry for the people of Russia and Ukraine and the world. In trying times such as this, I wish to utilize my knowledge and use this book as a way to spread hope, knowledge, and inspiration. Despite all odds, there are still ways to put yourself onto the path toward achieving your wildest dreams with personal, professional, or business excellence leading the way. In doing so, you can be the hope that others use to rise when everything around them forces them to fall.

This book is relevant for anyone who picks it up. If you're looking for a job, are currently unemployed, or are an overwhelmed professional, entrepreneur, or CEO experiencing burnout or stress, continuous improvement is at the forefront of the road to overcoming challenges and frustrations and achieving excellence. This is what I aim to teach everyone. It is never too late to make amends or grow from where you already stand.

Don't think of this as a miracle cure-all drug! I will provide you with the necessary tools and a blueprint for reaching your greatest potential. This book contains a set of personal excellence principles to help you face your challenges and the corresponding emotional responses and tackle them accordingly. By using a blend of scientific and spiritual teachings, you will get the best of both worlds! As they say, "Give a man a fish, and he eats for a day. Teach a man to fish, and he eats for a lifetime."

The next chapter will explain why it takes guts to climb to greater heights and how you can move forward on your specific path to attain your goals by striving for excellence in your chosen field. The only thing that differentiates you from other successful people is the willingness to do the actions and the work it takes to make your why create a significant difference in the lives of others. By the time you complete this book, you will have already set foot in the direction of change by eliminating the barriers that were created by society's mirrors.

Using a set of personal excellence principles, you can upgrade your mind's operating system, change your response to stimuli, and find the perfect equilibrium. You can evolve your mindset, alter your behaviors, and balance your perceptions.

On my continuous and ever-evolving personal excellence journey, I realized that things that matter the most must never be at the mercy of those who matter the least. To climb to greater heights, it's wise to have a set of principles of personal excellence to determine, examine, and modify our actions, behaviors, focus, and thoughts. It is why I synthesized years of learning into the Octagon of Excellence method, which you will be learning about in the follow-up chapters, and have a center point. The blueprint to your greatest potential consists of eight powerful, scientifically based principles for personal, professional, and business excellence. When used regularly, these principles will help you build a resilient mental framework and an easy-to-follow, step-by-step plan to face any adversity life throws at you as you climb to greater heights. They will guide you to meet any challenge head-on, adapt, behave, and act in ways that are best suited for the path of excellence you envision for your life.

The energy, the language, the meaning, and the power of each of the principles of personal excellence will become the foundation of any individual, relationship, professional, financial, or business transformation you seek and help you successfully deliver any task at hand.

Unleashing the true power of the Octagon of Excellence's principles requires you to acknowledge the role you play in the bigger scheme of life. The kind of thoughts you think and the type of language you use influence how life responds to the experiences you create in life. Remember, the principles only work if you choose to work with them every day.

What you will learn from this book will become your bread and butter. This is a book that you will read more than once, and you will probably have multiple bookmarks throughout!

2

IT TAKES GUTS TO CLIMB
GREATER HEIGHTS

Life is nothing short of a culmination of challenges. You have been faced with challenges from the moment you were born. Even as a baby, you overcame challenges by learning how to talk, crawl, and walk. One might think that challenges are simply something only humans face, but the truth is far from it. For the gazelles in the Serengeti, their challenge is learning how to walk within minutes of being born and acquiring enough nutrients such as vitamins and carbohydrates from plant-based diets. Challenges are a natural part of life for every living creature on our planet.

Most of us are fortunate enough not to worry about survival. We are born with a roof over our heads, food to eat, access to clean water, clothes, education, and so on. Yet, there are still a considerable number of humans who lack even these basic necessities. Before discussing the concept of challenges and how to face them, remember that the definition of a challenge varies from person to person. For some people, learning how to drive might be a challenge. For others, it's routine. However, this does not take away from the fact that it is a challenge in itself for them.

Without even realizing it, we are faced with challenges every day: a test in school, an important work project, resolving disputes between friends or family—the list is endless. However, most of us prefer to avoid these challenges; we study for the test later, reassign the project, or ignore the dispute until things fizzle out. We are all guilty of this. Accepting where we falter is the first step to understanding the importance of challenges.

It goes without saying that we are the masters of avoidance. To truly appreciate life for what it is, we need to face reality head-on—along with the challenges that follow. Once we are guided with a fundamental principle of personal excellence, we delve deeper into combatting life's many challenges. Buddhist teachings emphasize "wanting what you have." Learning to accept the challenges that you encounter is a crucial step of self-betterment and excellence. When we submit ourselves to the very reality of who we are, we allow ourselves ample opportunity to achieve what we can do.

All of this is a time-consuming process. It took me decades of changing cycles and facing adversities to reach where I am today. Had I not faced my challenges and succumbed to self-pity, I would still be homeless on the streets of London—or I would have been killed during the civil with my body buried somewhere.

There are no shortcuts to this; slow, incremental steps are the approach you need to take. One crucial thing is to practice gratitude. Even if your most significant challenge is being able to pay the bills on time, find ways to be grateful. There are millions of people who would love to be in your place. Practicing gratitude humbles you and provides you with a holistic view of people as a whole. By identifying your privilege, you can help those in need.

Accepting and taking on challenges is a daunting task, but to overcome any challenge, you have to face it head-on. You might fail a dozen times before you succeed. You can even learn from a baby! Do babies quit walking after falling once? No! A baby will fall dozens of times every day while it is learning to walk. For the baby, learning to walk is an unsurmountable challenge that needs to be addressed. The motivation behind their thinking is simple—they want to overcome their challenge and will not take no for an answer. Learn from babies! Be persistent, resilient, and willing! After all, life is nothing more than a series of learning encounters. Don't let anything undermine your ability to unlock your greatest potential and fulfill your ever-growing vision in life.

Before you continue reading, take a moment to write down the answer to the following questions:

- What does personal excellence mean to you?
- In what critical area of life do you want to achieve personal excellence? Is it spiritual, mental, emotional, physical, family, social, financial, or business or career? Be very specific.
- What specific challenges, difficulties, and fears do you need to overcome to climb to greater heights?
- What positive differences would overcoming those challenges, difficulties, and fears make in your personal, professional, social, financial, and business life?
- What is one new thing that could bring you a step closer to personal excellence?

Why Do People Give Up?

If people had retained their ingrained adaptability and resilience, I wouldn't have had to write this book! We all get bogged down by life and lose enthusiasm, faith, and sight; we've all been there. Often, we are merely procrastinating. Don't be quick to assume that this is simply due to laziness. Constant procrastination usually indicates not living by your hierarchy of authentic values. Some cases may be due to a more severe underlying mental health concern, such as anxiety and depression.

Another motivator for procrastination is wasting time on social media! I don't mean to demonize it in its entirety. In fact, I think it's a wonderful tool. However, it is wise to understand how they're not made to break this social media addiction that makes you mindlessly scroll through several apps for hours. Their very nature is to be addictive. The algorithm is designed to show you whatever interests you the most to keep you hooked. As long as you know that the scrolling is bottomless and that you will literally never run out of content, it can wait!

Do not confuse procrastination with taking a break from something you are doing that aligns with your authentic, values-driven excellence goals. The first is endless; the latter is mandatory! The significant difference between the two is that you know where your break starts and ends; there is a clear, defined definition. After helping thousands of people break free from procrastination, I observed that it shows up in sporadic, random ways and can last for hours if unchecked. It is vital to remember that procrastination is the result of not living in alignment with your authentic values and not seeing the hidden drawbacks and benefits of taking action. Whatever challenge you face, taking a break will often help clear your head and allow you to contemplate the situation from a fresh perspective.

Another barricade, when it comes to facing challenges, is people's perceptions. We fear failure and the judgment that comes with it. No matter how many failures I met, I've always thought of failure as a blessing in disguise. It continuously taught me how to evolve from my mistakes and expand my limits. If we fail to overcome challenges, we feel like failures. Individuals who go through infinite cycles of destruction and construction can fail a dozen challenges in life and still end up as the epitome of excellence.

A shining example of this is Jack Ma, the founder of Alibaba, one of the world's largest e-commerce platforms. He proudly states that he's been rejected from more than thirty jobs he applied for after failing out of university—even KFC didn't hire him! TO this day, he proudly wears his rejections and failures, highlighting just how glad he was that he failed but never gave up. From being unable to find any job to having a net worth of more than $36 billion, Jack Ma is an example of living life according to a set of personal excellence principles. You can use your failures for your betterment.

Judgments, if used wisely, can be very beneficial to you. Why? Because they can awaken your awareness to listen to yourself, sincerely. Frequently examine your daily priorities to make sure they align with your inner crucifix for personal excellence. Take failure as a stepping-stone to greatness and achieve excellence in your chosen area of life.

Another concern usually associated with failure is self-doubt. The first course of action is to accept it by acknowledging the role it plays in your ever-evolving life. There is no point thinking about what could have been. Instead, focus on your next course of action, "So this led to a dead-end, maybe I need to try a different approach." Improvise, adapt, overcome.

An Exercise for You

Please take a moment to write down everything that makes you give up, and next to each item, write down the reasons why you think it is so. Once you clarify what makes you give up, write down how this is a drawback and why it benefits you.

The Kinds of Experiences You Attract Depend on You

There is so much information about the universal laws that govern life: the law of vibration, compensation (fair exchange), polarity, correspondence, cause and effect, rhythm, relativity, gender, perpetual transmutation, karma, attraction, and divine oneness. Every adversity I overcame made me even more curious to learn why billions of people keep attracting what they don't want despite all of the knowledge of the above laws shared by some extraordinary teachers throughout history.

I spent years mastering the personal excellence principles you will be learning more about throughout the book to demystify our relationships with many of the laws that govern life. I did that because I never trusted my abilities, talents, looks, or luck, and I had no family, friends, or valuable industry connections when I first arrived in London to turn to for help. I studied what successful people did and tried to mimic that. I also researched what unsuccessful people did and avoided that.

While many things seem to differentiate those who are successful from those who aren't, I've noticed a clear difference that stands out the most: successful people are in flow with these universal laws. I had to ensure that my study and research included these laws and how they would increase my chances of making them work for me as it did for the successful people I studied. What I was learning was awakening me to embrace my quest to climb to greater heights, and it increased my faith in achieving what I desired. This discovery inspired me to create and embed the wisdom of these universal principles into the Octagon of Excellence Method that you will learn about in more detail in the following chapters. What could you achieve if you had a blueprint to unlock your potential? What if you had an easy-to-use method to break through perceived limits and achieve personal excellence in the areas of life that matter to you the most?

As you journey through life, it is important to remember how you make people feel with your deeds. It goes without saying just how far a good deed can take you. A good deed always rewards you in unimaginable ways, from helping someone with a flat tire or paying for someone's meal at the drive-through. By actively enveloping yourself in conscious thinking, gratitude, and random acts of kindness, you project this vibration out into the universe. In return, the universe aligns you with like-minded individuals who vibrate on a similar frequency. They often share the same sentiments as you. Good deeds harm no one and benefit everyone. On the other hand, bad deeds create karmic chains that tie you to negativity. The universe aligns you with individuals who vibrate with similar energy.

Have you ever been stuck in a rut, and despite overcoming whatever challenges you were presented with, you still failed to find inner satisfaction? For moments like these and everything else, make sure you know the principles of personal excellence that you want to lead your life by and make sure your actions, intentions, and authentic values are clear. The moment you make the intention to do something in alignment with your values and vision of excellence—to overcome challenges—cosmic energies put you on the path toward it. If, for example, you are expecting a promotion at work, it is wise to think, *I am grateful I got this promotion. I worked very hard for this!* That is better than thinking, *I hope I get this promotion! I don't want Emma to be my boss!* By speaking in the present tense and practicing a mindful way of thinking, we can vibrate in the energy of our desired outcomes.

Similarly, instead of harboring envy and resentments for those who have surpassed you, it is better to use them as inspiration, especially if you started together. *I'm grateful to Simon for getting this promotion instead of me. I'm sure he worked much harder than I did. I am grateful to have more time to learn and to set a higher benchmark for professional excellence!* That is better than thinking, *I can't believe Simon got a promotion rather than me! I deserved it! It doesn't matter if he is better than me or if he put in extra hours. I want it!* See what I mean?

Admirable intentions help cultivate excellent karma, and they also help shape your perceptions for the better, ultimately making you a better person who can handle challenges without grievances about the outcome.

How to Handle Challenges and Make Difficult Decisions

Just like Aristotle, through countless cycles of change and overcoming adversity after adversity, I concluded that excellence is not an act. It is a product of a habit of overcoming challenge after challenge. The more you evolve and grow as a person, the more complex, demanding, and stressful the challenges you will be facing will become. Ultimately, if you do not stay on top of them, they'll make you doubt your abilities and lose sight of your goals.

We are faced with innumerable challenges every day, but we overcome them with ease and without a second thought. Driving to work or the grocery store may seem mundane, but when you were learning to drive, it was a challenge. Every novice driver has insecurities and uneasiness when they drive; they are working on overcoming their challenges. Do you consider driving a challenge anymore? Congratulations! This is just one of the many daily challenges you have overcome without even realizing it! It is another step toward excellence!

You may falter many times while achieving your goals. There are going to be many bumps or potholes that you're going to encounter along this journey. Is it going to be easy? Unlikely. Is overcoming it going to be satisfying? Most definitely! You are not alone when you face your challenges. Humanity has been facing challenges that come from infinite cycles of creation and destruction since the advent of humans themselves! Our hunter-gatherer forefathers had to trek for hundreds of miles in search of food and water. Had they been unsuccessful in doing so, I wouldn't be writing this book—and you wouldn't be reading it!

Challenges come with a surge of uncertainty. Ancient humans had to watch out for predators, poisonous food, natural disasters, famine, and more. Although most people do not have to worry about these things anymore, everyone has challenges. Every life cycle is a different experience, and whatever you're going through is exclusive to you. I plan to help you overcome these and any other challenges you might encounter in your life's journey.

A way to visualize overcoming challenges is to think of yourself climbing a steep hill. The more complicated the challenge is, the steeper it is. However, right at the top is a plateau—a place where you can rest and recuperate. If you make that push and reach the top, you can take a much-needed break and look down to see your progress. The only difference is that the hill goes on forever! It has multiple facets and varying heights and extremes. The only thing keeping you from achieving greater heights is you.

Whether it's an important work assignment or a difficult school exam—anything of importance and equal difficulty—overcoming your day-to-day challenges will help you stay centered and calm under pressure. Think back to the driving example. Do you stress out at the thought of having to drive on roads? If you've been driving for a while, your answer will most definitely be no!

Challenges reveal your true character. No one is perfect—and that's a great thing! Being perfect signifies achieving the pinnacle—there's nothing more to gain. However, realizing that we are flawed and subject to our highs and lows highlights that we can continuously improve. This is not just limited to us as individuals. It extends throughout every facet of our lives, including work, school, and friends.

All of us have weaknesses and flaws. The first sign of growth is that you can self-reflect; you can pick out where you lack and where you excel and work on those parts of your personality. Doing so will hone your skills and diligently guide you down the path of excellence that is created by your ever-evolving values, mission, and vision.

Contrary to popular belief, success isn't a one-hit wonder! Most people think it's possible to be successful by developing a revolutionary idea, which is true. However, the crucial detail they want to miss out on is how hard work and dedication are intertwined throughout the process! Bill Gates is a college dropout, but he went to Harvard. He applied himself throughout his school career to gain admission to Harvard. He also worked tirelessly to make Microsoft the tech behemoth it is today.

My life can serve as an example to everyone reading this. I had to survive a civil war, fight homelessness, and struggle with poverty and a series of mental, emotional, and physical health issues. If I had kept to my self-destructive ways, I wouldn't have been an award-winning author of many books. In fact, I doubt I'd even be alive at this point. Nevertheless, I understood the real meaning of personal excellence through my struggles and envisioned this fact. Despite the challenges I faced, I used the same principles of personal excellence you will be learning to make me believe that I was destined for greatness and achieve it. This simple act of manifesting put it out into the universe, and the universe always responds to what you send out with your vibration.

How you face the challenges in your life might be significantly different than how Bill Gates or I did, but there are a few tips and tricks that remain constant for all challenges. Curious? They're right around the corner!

One Decision Can Change Your Life

As I travel globally to consult with clients, train groups, and be interviewed on TV and radio, I am often asked what it takes to change one's life. My answer is always the same: "It takes one decision." This often sparks curiosity in those who ask.

We make countless decisions every day, and each one of them creates a new reality. For instance, if two friends arrange to meet in one place, they need to decide to create that reality. If, however, one of the friends makes a different decision, that reality in meeting in that one place would never manifest.

Obviously, certain decisions hold more significance than others, such as what you choose to eat for breakfast or how your company handles its transactions. Consciously and unconsciously, we make decisions that affect our lives—whether we actively want them to or not. It's like rolling a snowball down a hill.

Every decision sets off a chain reaction of events, which is known as the butterfly effect. Perhaps you gave one of your employees a bonus for their continuous hard work. Although you might not know this, maybe they were in a financial bind, and you helped them immensely. What did you do? You simply valued someone for their worth, but you gained positive karma in the process. The opposite also holds true. You might fire an employee for their mistakes, unbeknownst to the internal and external factors that led to their underperformance.

Let me share an example from my own life. I have been running my own business for a few years. However, like the rest of the world, my business suffered a significant blow after the pandemic hit. I could have given up and relied on the government's financial aid or adapted to the change. I chose the latter. I made a decision. The first thing I did was adjust my goals, set new priorities, and clarify my vision of excellence during this period. I eliminated most of my other face-to-face consulting work. I adapted to the new environment shaped by countless government decisions to contain the coronavirus pandemic. I utilized the energy I would have otherwise used in person in an online manner.

My consulting sessions, seminars, interviews, and everything else were being conducted online from the comfort of my home. With the travel restrictions in place, I could not catch a flight to travel to my clients. Under normal circumstances, I would travel to exotic locations worldwide to teach my five- or ten-day business and self-mastery class, a custom-made VIP coaching program for visionaries, high achievers, leaders, and business owners: "Vital Planning for Elevated Living."

This decision changed my perceptions. I realized I didn't need to be physically present to help my clients overcome their personal, professional, or business challenges. My books, courses, virtual consultations, and Vital Planning for Elevated Living had been selling regularly. I could use all of the travel time I would typically use to plan for the journey in times of extreme uncertainty and global meltdowns.

I clarified my vision and updated my business and my financial, marketing, and sales processes. Consequently, my mind was not focused on the "Armageddon doom-scenario" the media and conspiracy theorists want you to believe. I adapted fast and decreased my workload dramatically. I used this free time to keep growing my business, learn new skills, do Zoom talks for nonprofit organizations, and spend quality time with my partner, family, and friends. It helped me support several of my clients who had COVID.

Now that I had more time, I realized that my heart was calling me to evolve my sense of purpose beyond what I was doing, and the decision to utilize the stay-at-home lockdown initiative focused me on writing three more books. I wrote *The Unfakeable Code®* to raise awareness about the negative mental, emotional, and physical impact of living an inauthentic live. Furthermore, it promotes authenticity as a powerful tool to solve emerging global social, economic, business, and leadership problems. In creating another one-of-a-kind method, I knew that people from all walks of life would be called to use it to redefine themselves in adversity, take back control, lead authentically, and live freely on their terms.

Essentially, I found new ways to contribute to the world, irrespective of what income my consultancy business and my retreats generated. My clear vision of positively impacting the lives of one billion people makes me crave a greater sense of connection, contribution, and personal excellence. I decided to write more books, and I published "Take Off the Mask, Your Soul is Waiting: Poetry Selections that Quench Your Thirst for Growth, Love, and Wisdom" in *Novum #10*. I wanted my poetry to be the inspiration you need to be brave, scared, or sad and to radically embrace and truly be grateful for your imperfections. At the beginning of my entrepreneurial journey, my mind could not conceive of that, and I never thought it was possible to achieve it.

Over the seemingly endless months of lockdown, I received offers to speak in various international forums online. I did interviews for TV, radio, podcasts, magazines, blogs, Facebook Lives, joint-venture leadership, and business-building webinars. Not traveling as much and using personal excellence principles helped me adapt quickly to the challenges COVID-19 brought into our lives.

My first paid speaking gig was for a tech company back in 2012, but it felt meaningful to speak at virtual events for free and inspire as many people as I could to not let the pandemic overshadow their quest for excellence.

I felt fulfilled in seeing others' hopes light up. The intention of giving value freely and seeing others happy created a lot of business. Many people attending those online events booked private sessions, and some even signed up to my yearly virtual coaching program and booked themselves on my Vital Planning Advanced Life and Business Mastery Coaching Program. Since I understand how difficult it is to have everything taken from you, I used a portion of my free time to freely help those going through hardship.

It is essential to realize that money isn't the root of happiness; your sense of purpose goes beyond meeting your existential needs. Sure, it's helpful to have money to meet your primary and ever-growing needs, but true contentment comes from within. No expensive gifts can change that. Remember, those who give freely receive freely, and those who pay for the value they receive end up being paid generously.

Looking back, I can see how many of my problems began in primary school and when I spent two years in the hospital. I was in and out of a life-support machine due to collapsed lungs, a heart murmur, and the various illnesses that followed. The many drugs I was given contributed to my becoming overweight and overdeveloped. I was bullied and physically harassed and verbally abused by other kids. Furthermore, seeing your mother, father, older sisters, and older brother being abused gives you little hope that your life will be better. Since that time was so traumatic for me, I revel in the opportunity to speak to those who may be struggling to break through challenges and see a clear vision of their purposeful vision of excellence.

This led me to a tough decision. Would I listen to the instinct that told me to try to make sense of the global uncertainty the pandemic and the raging war in Ukraine brought to us? Would I listen to the intuition that told me to stay unplugged while writing this book, virtually consulting clients, and spending time with my partner?

Would I do what comes naturally to me? I've used various ways to remain on track, stay on a path to excellence, and inspire positive action in the lives of one billion people? Would I keep advising clients virtually and help whenever I could online? Would I step outside the world of the lockdown and war and onto a path of personal excellence and see where it would lead?

One seems to involve a lot more certainty. I feel fulfilled when I'm assisting more people globally. Coaching, mentoring, and teaching my five-day transformative business and life-mastery program helps more people climb to greater heights, create the breakthroughs they seek, and keep growing to their fullest potential. I sometimes feel frustrated that I'm spending so much time alone on my computer.

I have been helping my clients with a million unknowns. What's next for them if it isn't online? How do they pick one of the many ideas they shared with me? How can the principles in the following chapters help them bring it to fruition? How do they know that what they choose will work out, and if it doesn't, will they regret not going the other way?

The answer is they don't, can't, and won't. We can never know for sure when we make a decision that it's going to pan out. No one thought we would face a pandemic like this or the invasion of Ukraine. All we can do is follow our most vital calling and then trust that the future will wake us up and enrich our lives in one way or another.

Many of my clients have been struggling with personal and business decisions recently. in the next chapter, I share the wisdom of the Octagon of Excellence method. Why did I create it? How can it help you on your never-ending journey through overcoming adversity after adversity, challenge after challenge, doubt after doubt, fear after fear, and stress after stress?

The principles embedded in this one-of-a-kind method are endless. Use them to clarify your vision for excellence in any of the eight critical areas of life, get unstuck, improve your relationships, grow your teams, and commit to embracing the challenges and blessings that will come as a result. You can even use them to help you in your decision-making process, strengthen your will, grow your wealth, influence the world, and upgrade your psychology in alignment with what you want to achieve in any of the critical areas of life. The actionable steps embedded in the method can help you make difficult decisions quickly.

There are consequences for every course of action. It is wise to decide which course of action will be best first and foremost for you and then for everyone else. Seeing the situation objectively from all angles can help you decide wisely. Think about how the decision will make you feel when you're eighty, ninety, or one hundred years old. Following what you are learning will put the difficult decision into perspective (maybe it's not as big a deal as you think it is). Secondly, it will help you make an informed and wise decision for the long term rather than just for instant gratification.

To give you every chance possible to succeed in your journey to climb to greater heights and achieve the kind of personal excellence your body, mind, heart, and soul are capable of attaining, be sure to pay extra attention to the next chapter.

3

THE OCTAGON OF EXCELLENCE

> We are what we repeatedly do. Excellence,
> then, is not an act, but a habit.
> —Aristotle

As someone born in a culture where you are treated as a minority, like an inferior person, and not given opportunities just because you are of a different caste or creed, I know how it feels to be persistently told you are not good enough or that you are not destined for excellence.

What if I told you an octagon, a simple, eight-sided shape, could help change your life?

The Octagon of Excellence, the blueprint to achieving your greatest potential, deals with this very concept. Gaining a comprehensive understanding of how this works will provide you with a scientific and holistic insight into the individual principles of excellence, which are described in more detail in the upcoming chapters.

The symbolic meaning of the Octagon of Excellence deals with embracing the ongoing eight cycles of life:

- transition
- regeneration
- focus
- rebirth
- balance
- service
- unity
- infinity

These eight factors play a crucial role in your ever-evolving quest for excellence. Each of the eight principles of personal excellence will ensure you can embrace and overcome the challenges of transitional cycles that happen for your growth. No matter what challenge you may be facing, it is there to bring awareness that you are ready to transition into something better.

Through every life challenge, you will experience some form of regeneration. As you learn to overcome more challenges, you will focus even more your energy and actions on high-priority things. Each pain will become the seed that takes you through a rebirthing experience, like a phoenix triumphantly emerging from the ashes. You will start to observe how everything in your internal and outer reality has a hidden order that keeps things in balance.

Your newfound awareness will turn all you have learned into even more excellent service for others. You start to see every hardship that tries to break you as the teacher who unifies you to all you are and perceives you as not. Eventually, your intuition will guide you to unlock the power and the infinite wisdom existing in you and in life that is hidden from your awareness until you become a stable conduit to channel it for the greater good of self and others. The Octagon of Excellence's symbolic meaning and associated eight principles will become the crucifix, the Northern Star, from which you can correct your course to excellence and achieve your fullest potential.

I am not alone in using the octagon as a directional symbol on your path to excellence or even a stepping-stone to help you reach greater heights. The octagon is found in baptisteries as a symbol representing eternal life, likely because the number eight is symbolic of renewal. The octagon's use and prevalence have been widely observed throughout history from the octagonal domes in the Hagia Sophia to the Basilica of San Vitale. We see further religious architectural connections when we recognize many sacred buildings (churches, mosques, and temples) were designed with octagonal structures supporting a dome on top. Even from an architectural point of view, the octagon provides a tremendously stable structure.

This interplay between the circle (dome) and square (found in the angular octagon) speaks of the transitional dance between earth and space (heaven). The circle is symbolic of the heavens (eternity/infinity), and the angularity of the square is symbolic of earthly presence. Many ancient orders were aware of this amazingly profound concept, including the Masons, and took the time to design their places of worship with no symbolic detail unmissed.

Having learned how to use a compass to find my way to various destinations from a very young age, I like looking at the symbolism of the octagon from a navigational standpoint. I like to imagine each point of the octagon as one among the four cardinal directions and the four intermediate points. I occasionally use this imagery in meditations in conjunction with the Buddhist concept of the eightfold path:

- right thought
- right word
- right concentration
- right mindfulness
- right view
- right action

- right effort
- right livelihood

The above order is slightly different from the one described in Buddhism. I created this specific order to make more sense for my scientific and engineering mind to follow, implement, and use daily. It took me years to demystify what the Buddhist concept meant in terms of my excellence and life purpose. As I overcame challenge after challenge, I realized how important it is to have the proper thought, right word, concentration, mindfulness, view, action, effort, and livelihood. Without these eight things, your life experiences will be full of judgments, pain, and roadblocks. I am sharing them with you to make your journey through the ups and downs of life more acceptable.

In studying various life disciplines and philosophies, I realized the power of symbols, why symbolic meanings matter, and why everything from ancient religions to modern-day brands uses them. The cross, the moon, the star, the multiarmed goddess Kali, the four-headed Suantevitus, the lamb, the dove, the wheel, Apple, IBM, Microsoft, Nike, Starbucks, Metaverse, Tesla, and so on are all created to carry a specific message and create memory, meaning, mental state, and momentum.

This realization helped me coin the term "*The Five Ms of Brand Excellence*", which ended up becoming a talk and a seminar that I started to teach to the many business owners I coached. We used this five-step process to help them create a powerful brand story, carry an emotional message, and build momentum that creates a long-lasting memory in their customers' minds. We link it to a meaningful cause and design a brand that creates transformative mental states in people's minds. Many of us love brands because of the way they make us feel. They can make you feel beautiful, happy, joyful, rich, or powerful.

I helped one of my clients clarify and partially ghostwrite her new book. She was one of the many clients who used the Five Ms of

Brand Excellence during her five-day Vital Planning Life Mastery retreat. It helped her create a personal brand that she could connect with and carry her soul's voice. I used it to help her bring together years of learning and helping others into a series of relationship-focused books. In January 2019, with tears of gratitude, she said, "Tony, my precious, you are the first person to see right through me. I feel listened to, heard, and seen for the care, love, and wisdom I have to offer to others. For the first time in my life, I feel seen."

I felt very honored. Since then, she has invested a lot of time, energy, and money in keeping her pledge to do quarterly Vital Planning for Elevated Living Advanced Life Mastery retreats. In investing in being privately coached by me in locations worldwide, I used all I had mastered to grow her business by ten times in less than three years.

Was it luck? No, it was a combination of our commitment to personal excellence, to learning, and to doing the focused work that would achieve the kind of results she had never dreamed of. Most people seeing photos and videos of us in locations worldwide, including London, Northern Macedonia, Switzerland, Mexico, Dominican Republic, Kosovo, the United States, and Turkey, would assume all she does is relax. The truth is far from that.

As the coronavirus pandemic started to shut the world in 2020, I suddenly found myself in a lockdown with plenty of free time. I decided to use what was once travel time to learn new things, continue with my research, and offer more virtual coaching to many more incredible clients from around the world. Like me, many of my clients, took what was happening as an opportunity to adapt, create breakthroughs and clarity, and plan to turn around their personal, professional, and business lives. The Octagon of Excellence is a solution to help others who want to back from feeling frustrated, uncertain, stressed, and out of control.

I spent countless nights sifting all I have learned and taught others into eight principles for personal excellence that people can use to unlock their potential and the mind's true power. To climb to greater heights is in your destiny if you choose it. All you have to do is be clear about what you want to see once you are at the top of your mountain; your purpose and the vision of excellence will become more transparent than ever.

Symbols and principles have an unseen force, and they can carry on your idea and life philosophy for centuries. It is why most people know the symbols for some of the main religions and brands. Some people even go to the extent of operating by certain principles.

The foundations of the symbolization process lie in the areas of the unconscious and the conscious of experience and thought and intuition, sense perception, and imagination. From these arises the structure of brand and religious symbolism. Sensation and physiological and psychological processes participate in the formation of the symbol.

Symbols can make you feel and focus better, and they can help you improve your memory, change your state, and draw strength from the spirit and the divine when times are tough. A set of principles can help you shape and shift existing mind paradigms into a clear vision of excellence.

For many people, an octagon may trigger images of stop signs or family-sized pizzas. For me, it triggers a picture of an octagonal mirror that my mind uses to see many sides and angles to every situation. I opened myself to learn that an octagon is also the MIT Technology Hackers Association (THA) symbol:

> The eight sides of the octagon represent eight aspects of human endeavor; initially, these coincided to some extent with the areas mentioned inside the little dome at MIT: arts, agriculture, science, etc.

Whatever specific definition one would like is fine, providing the set covers most categories of what people do with their brains. Having spent some time observing the center of the octagon symbol, I noticed how it represents the generalists' activities, bordered on the edges by the above realms of the specialists. The solid crossbar in the octagon signifies creativity as the unifying element in all of these areas. The trim lines paralleling the crossbar are intended to represent the necessity of intellectual discipline that hold it all together. Now that is something worth adopting and remembering, wouldn't you agree?

Many years ago, during a personal vision of excellence workshop, a group of authors, entrepreneurs, and business owners was looking to grow all eight key areas of life. In one of the exercises, I had the attendees visualize their perfect "sanctuary," a place they could go mentally and be free and safe. My sanctuary was constructed of marble, wood, and octagon-shaped glass with colorful windows on every side.

I have no idea how or why the octagon shape came about back then. It just came to me seemingly out of nowhere, but I knew it had to have some meaning behind it. One day, my house, which is my sanctuary, would be an octagon. It made perfect sense.

As the years went by, I found myself creating many things that included number eight. I wrote about the eight critical areas of life in *A Path to Wisdom*, and I ended up purchasing a two-bedroom flat on the eighth floor. Some may say it's a coincidence, but I say it's a result of conscious creation fueled by a clear vision and daily inspired actions.

As the number of people I coached kept increasing, I realized how the issues I was helping them overcome were part of the ever-evolving octagonal cycles that we go through as we empower all of the eight critical areas of life: mental, emotional, physical, spiritual, relationship, social, business, and financial. Whether you realize it or not, intuitively, you strive to be all you can be. Committing to and investing your time in continuous learning is essential to your ever-evolving transformation into personal excellence.

Meaning of the Number Eight

Why eight principles? The meaning of the number eight rolls into our consciousness with the momentum of all the numbers that come before it. Numbers play an essential role in your brain's multifaceted activities. I wanted to step out of the aspects of structure and perfection in the number seven, which paved the way for another evolution in the magic of numbers and birthed the importance of the number eight. There are the unavoidable eight cycles of life.

As an evolved child of structure, the number eight seeks balance with non-structure. The number eight is about infinite cycles, revolutions, and progress gained on the invisible level, which is something each of us undergoes as we take on challenge after challenge.

The number eight's most obvious symbolic tell is its written Arabic form ("8"). When we recognize its voluptuous curves, we also identify the lemniscate or infinity symbol. This symbol deals with balance, time, and the recycling travel path of energy.

Einstein was able to derive a law that we still use today, governed by one of the most straightforward but most powerful equations ever to be written down: $E = mc^2$.

There are only three parts to Einstein's most famous energy equation: E, or energy, which represents the total energy of the system, m, or mass, which is related to energy by a conversion factor, and c^2, which is the speed of light squared. You are energy; thus, how you choose to focus your energy matters.

These questions can help demystify the meaning of the number eight:

- When you observe the number eight, what thoughts and feelings come up for you?
- What can you learn from the cyclical patterns in your life that can move you into inspiration?

- Is time your ally or your enemy? If it's your foe, how do you resolve that conflict?
- How can you maintain the balance you seek?
- Can you trust that the cycle of life will provide for all your needs?

These questions offer depth to this number, and I encourage you to use the number eight in your daily practices and meditations to fire up new brain synapses and engage in conscious activities that tap into your rhythmical, cyclical nature.

There are many exercises you can do. One that you can do this right now is through breathing. Interestingly, the number eight has an arithmetic correlation to the letter H, which is associated with the lungs because ancient alchemists observed the lungs look somewhat like an H.

Take a moment, close your eyes, and start to envision the cyclical path of breath moving through your lungs and body in a figure-eight (or infinity symbol) pattern. This lulls the critical mind, engages the spirit in a softer activity, and ignites our deeper selves by flipping on an intuitive switch that turns on depth within you that is both alpha, omega, and omni. Don't skip this exercise. Give it a try. It's effective and pretty amazing.

As you continue to work on the meaning of the number eight, consider the following key points related to this number. They resemble a fusion of Western and Eastern philosophies that use the eight previously mentioned concepts:

- Transition. This may show up in the form of transitioning from working a nine-to-five job to becoming a full-time entrepreneur. For others, it could be going from being single to starting to date, moving in with a partner, and having children.

- Regeneration. Nature is in a constant cycle of renewal, and so are we. This life cycle may show up in the form of new clothes, jobs, relationships, friends, places to live, customers, or businesses.
- Focus. Where focus goes, energy flows. No matter what goal you have, remaining focused on the end in mind will eventually get you there.
- Rebirth. Each time you overcome a hurdle, master something, own a trait, learn a new skill, or travel to a new destination you always wanted to visit, you are going through the experience of not knowing to knowing, of giving birth to a more integrated you.
- Balance. It's easy to tip the scale of eternal or external balance. You can forget the wholeness of who you are and shift your focus to negative self-talk. Learn to do things that maintain this inner and outer equilibrium daily.
- Service. No matter what you do, you are benefitting someone. The more people you serve, the more recognition you will get—and the wealthier and more content you will become. Focus on the value you bring on the table and the benefits of having a heart of service.
- Unity. In your divine nature, you are inseparable from all that is. Make it a life mission to transcend those inner separations caused by judgment and embrace the oneness of all that is. Daily work of integrating skewed perception, so your authentic being can emerge stronger each day.
- Infinity. To find the beauty in you, strive to continuously invest your energy, time, and money in building the greatest asset: you. Your continuous development will keep empowering you to look for answers to the most significant questions in the infinity of your divinity.

Visually, the number eight illustrates:

- cell mitosis: reminiscent of the process of joining, dividing, evolving
- Lemniscate: (infinity) symbol
- eyes: (tipped on its side) seeking out higher wisdom

Common associations with the meaning of the number eight:

- colors: brown, red
- letters: h, q, and z
- Qabalah symbol: cheth
- astrological: Uranus

Those who resonate with the vibration of eight are incredibly successful at something, particularly in business, where success relies on a time that allows progress to unfold. If this is you, you will see trends and the bigger picture and ride a wave to your significant gains. Conversely, you know when to pull out of engagements that don't work for you. You have a unique sense and strong intuition that give insight into things' cyclical nature. You may be even great at games of chance, stock markets, and anything that deals with playing the odds or working with statistics. Most importantly, you look into infinity to find answers to every challenge life throws at you.

What Limits You Is What You Believe Isn't True

All of the above symbolic meanings will make sense to you as you start to apply the principles of the Octagon of Excellence in your everyday life. They are not something you need to acquire, and they are there for you to use on your ever-evolving, awakening journey through life.

You may consider this method an extraordinary tool that upgrades your mental and emotional faculties and helps you build an agile mind and a grateful heart. As your mind starts to expand and evolve, you naturally will become even more aware, confident, and intuitive. You will be in a position to dissolve and resolve any of the perceived fears, pains, and losses every life challenge presents to you with greater confidence and certainty.

It's an undeniable scientific fact that your brain is programmable. You will be going through continuous transition cycles, regeneration, focus, rebirth, balance, service, unity, and infinity throughout life. Therefore, whatever program your mind may be running at any moment contains relevant and outdated thinking and codes developed through centuries of evolution. Your mind's data, information, and memories start in the womb of your mother.

Acknowledging this truth of life alone elevates your thinking significantly, builds your confidence, and energizes your body and mind. It also creates an extraordinary mind that ensures it holds itself accountable to the eight personal excellence principles you are about to discover.

Throughout history, scholars, psychologists, scientists, philanthropists, and philosophers have developed knowledge, tools, and methods that allowed changes and corrections to be made to the mind's programming. We can use what we learn to put us on a path to excellence. You can be all that your voids are calling you to be.

Whatever the approach, it needs to satisfy some fundamental rules. With my "scientist, business and human behavior specialist" hat, I created the Octagon of Excellence's eight mind-evolving, confidence-building, resilience- and strength-developing, genius-enhancing business and self-mastery transforming principles:

1. To break free from ambiguity, clarify what you want, why you want it, and when you want it.
2. To awaken your astronomical vision, commit to something bigger than yourself.

3. To build your resilience, immediately confront any issues that arise.
4. To make mistakes is human; ensuring you correct them awakens your excellence.
5. To learn better and more efficient and more effective ways to create results, consult with an expert willfully.
6. To grow on the inside and expand on the outside, learn to collaborate mindfully.
7. To unleash the power of gratitude, graciously give and accept compliments.
8. To change your physiology and strengthen your psychology, continuously celebrate small wins.

The above eight principles of the Octagon of Excellence are based on eight actionable verbs that, when used in harmony with your vision for excellence, can help you clarify, commit, confront, correct, consult, collaborate, compliment, and celebrate the good and the bad you encounter on your journey to attaining personal excellence. It is a tried and scientifically proven series of actions that can help you create a new state of being and the clarity required to make the personal excellence plan in any critical area of life you wish to enhance.

When the principles of the Octagon of Excellence are utilized in business, it signifies the following:

1. Less confusion, gossip, and stress. Improves engagement and increases productivity.
2. Enhanced collaborative team spirit that is driven by a shared vision and values.
3. Improves business performance by mindfully addressing and dissolving conflicts.
4. Promotes learning and development by using mistakes as lessons and instigators for business growth, evolution, and transformation.

5. It unlocks vast unexplored human capital by investing in using an Octagon of Excellence-trained consultant.
6. It creates an intelligent and sustainable workforce through shared learning, skills, and resources.
7. It transforms organizational culture by promoting appreciation, diversity, equality, fairness, and gratitude.
8. It celebrates small wins that energize and inspire employees and promote personal and professional excellence.

The more you practice and repeat these eight principles of personal excellence, the more you increase the chances of meeting every challenge life throws at you with clarity, confidence, and creativity. The more your organization or business thrives, the more you will start to unlock life's miracles in the terra incognita.

Consistently using these eight principles of personal excellence will help you train and nurture your body and continuously upgrade your psychology in alignment with the growth your mind, heart, and soul are seeking from you. Use them to excel in your personal, familial, social, professional, financial, and business lives.

Every roadblock you encounter in life is a guide that can turn your inner discord and chaos into outer order and success. The following chapters were written in a way that artfully, metaphorically, and scientifically teach you to overcome adversity by using a set of principles to unleash the infinite wisdom you possess.

As *Star Trek*'s Captain Jean Luc Picard would say, "To boldly go where no man has gone before!" Use the Octagon of Excellence principles to help you chart a precise life plan you can follow and go from where you are to where you want to be in life.

As you read, you will start to awaken your God-given dormant intelligence and inspire those around you to do the same. You'll come to understand how your low-level thinking is no longer serving you if you are aiming to reach high and be excellent in your chosen area of growth, expertise, or profession.

By embracing the ocean of wisdom that lives in you and the interconnectedness of life, you'll realize how to draw practical knowledge that helps you climb to greater heights and thrive in every critical area of life.

The more often you use these eight principles of excellence, the more you stimulate your mind to grow and awaken the senses you thought you never had. You start to observe people, events, and internal and external challenges with objectivity, a new pair of lenses that spot opportunities to do more extraordinary things in life.

The more obstacles you start to overcome, the more ways you'll find to solve problems, serve more people, have more fun, and increase your health, wealth, and vision. Overcoming things that challenge you with certainty, confidence, and courage will feel more natural.

Many of your default neural networks are being activated as your mind wanders from one chapter to another, from one story to another, from one metaphor to another, and from one principle of excellence to another. Other dormant brain systems will be activated each time you answer the many quality questions you will find throughout this book, bringing greater clarity to your life.

Distinctly different neuro networks are activated during exercises designed for you, including the recommended actions, principles, guided meditations, and accompanying online courses. If you choose to, you can consult with me privately, book a consultation or a business strategy session, or attend one of my global talks and seminars.

Practicing all that you are learning daily will help you see how adversity plays an essential part in your ever-evolving purpose in life. You'll be mystified by the new levels of awareness that became accessible to you.

Achievements that once seemed impossible suddenly become possible, and so will your experiences of feeling free, light, triumphant, and peaceful. The expansion of your consciousness beyond the self-imposed limits will teach you many other valuable lessons.

Choosing your specific path to excellence becomes the foundation and the lens through which you create, examine, and expand your reality. Through every life cycle, you will start to acknowledge the presence of love in all matters, living and nonliving. You slowly shift to a more favorable reality where you have the freedom to do what you once could not.

Whether or not you realize this, your experience of the world—and, thus, your behavior—will be strongly influenced by daily using the principles embedded in the Octagon of Excellence. Your upgraded mind's programs will help you develop a more empowering perspective for all that life throws at you, including the people who will challenge and support you.

The way you observe the reality you may find yourself in will continuously shift and change—and so will your attitudes and perceptions toward yourself and others. Your commitment to climb to greater heights will start to attract new opportunities, inspire people, and create situations and experiences that will bring you one step closer to your path to excellence.

Your pursuit of excellence will undoubtedly close some doors with people you once knew and open many doors with people who inspire you to attain the freedom and transformation you seek and the success you wish to bring into your life. Adopting, learning, and using each principle of personal excellence daily will help you own your power, grow your worth, and lead your life with a newfound mindful and transcendental awareness.

The Octagon of Excellence is about using a fusion of scientific and holistic principles derived from thirty years of learning, study, and experience to fundamentally transform how you approach challenges, fears, and the uncertainty that comes on a journey to climbing greater heights and reaching for excellence. Every critical area of your life—spiritual, mental, emotional, physical, relationship, social, business, and wealth—will go through infinite cycles of change, revolution, expansion, balance, and perception transformation. Repetition of those cycles and with the principles of personal excellence will ensure that you keep evolving, so you can freely rule in the seat of your soul's kingdom: your heart.

Ready for more? Let's continue.

4

ADIOS, MENTAL CONFUSION: THE SOURCE OF AVOIDABLE HEADACHES

Principle 1: To break free from ambiguity, clarify what you want, why you want it, and when you want it.

Have you ever tried thinking about something but just couldn't? It's happened to all of us. Whether we were taking an important exam about something we've studied for weeks or months, we draw a blank on the day of the exam. At work, it happens while delivering an important pitch or negotiating a fruitful deal. You might have stumbled with your words, "uh," "um," "ugh," becoming the norm. You beat around the bush, but you can't hit the nail on the head.

When we're unable to think clearly, it's often paired with feeling disorientated with a loss of focus. A pretty accurate way to visualize confusion is via this viral image that gained notoriety on the internet in 2020:

Here's a fun challenge for you; can you name a single object in this image? Everything looks quite familiar, yet what is it?

That is what I believe is what confusion looks like. What confuses us? Let's start with a biological view.

Mental Confusion: What Is It?

Confusion is a symptom that doesn't allow you to think clearly. For the majority of us, confusion is an occasional occurrence. In extreme cases, it's referred to as delirium. Prolonged instances of confusion can be part of early onset dementia. Confusion causes a person to lose the ability to perform regular motor functions, memory, judgment, behavior, or all of the above. Specific symptoms of confusion include:

- Long pauses during a speech, can't collect thoughts.
- Incoherent speech, mumbling or rambling out of nowhere.

- Losing awareness of what you're doing, spacing out.
- Forgetting what a task is while doing it, going blank while working.
- Sudden changes in emotional state, feeling anxious or agitated out of the blue.

What causes these symptoms? If it's not a concussion—in that case, you need prompt medical attention—the leading cause is dehydration! About 60 percent of an adult's body is water, so dehydration can cause havoc.

The brain sends electric signals to all parts of the body in a very simplified manner. These signals pass through synapses, which are small gaps between neurons. When you're dehydrated, there aren't enough electrolytes—water contains these in small quantities—to facilitate this "transfer" of information, causing the aforementioned symptoms.

Medicine can also confuse us. Short-term cases of confusion can be a sign of nutritional imbalances. Some of the most significant causes of mental confusion are doubt, fear, and living according to other people's expectations. The latter is the most widespread problem that millions of people experience, so let what you are learning to assist you in clarifying what causes your mental fog and the actions you can take to overcome it.

Obtaining Clarity

Clarity is the difference between a heavy fog and a cloudless sky; you don't need to be a meteorologist to know that it's easier and safer to travel in the latter. Keeping the importance of attaining clarity in perspective, it's only logical for it to be the first principle. Let's learn just how we can obtain clarity by utilizing some aspects of it.

Taking 100 Percent Responsibility

On your journey to obtaining clarity, you need to come to terms with your past actions. It would be best if you stopped letting things drag you down. Resolve any qualms or dilemmas that have been in the back of your mind.

Taking responsibility doesn't just include your mistakes. Learn to take responsibility for your achievements as well! Be proud of what you've achieved and put yourself on a path to clear your mind so you can look forward to what the future holds. The key is to transform your perception of responsibility into "having a response-ability" and decide to establish clarity of the next steps.

Discerning What Aids in Clarity and What Doesn't

Specific actions, practices, behaviors, and words radiate positivity and attract it toward you. For example, what will make you more refreshed (grant you more clarity): getting a good eight hours of sleep, waking up in the morning to exercise, and having a healthy, balanced meal or going to sleeping at 3:00 a.m., waking up at 7:00 a.m. for work, and only having coffee for breakfast. It's a no-brainer! By adopting beneficial hobbies, you set yourself on the course of attaining clarity.

Practice Values-Aligned Goal-Setting Strategies

Imagine you're going on a road trip to a destination a thousand miles away. Before this grand adventure, do you just set off without preparation? Do you check the tire pressure, radiator fluid, engine oil, and all the main components of your car before embarking on this journey?

Stephen Hawking said, "Work gives you meaning and purpose, and life is empty without it." Utilize this mindset! If the first thought that comes to your mind is "I want to, but what if," you are overthinking. You don't need to find picture-perfect goals and aspirations; you just need to start. Get the ball rolling and make decisions as you go. To further assist you, here are some everyday goals to stimulate your thinking and incorporate into your life:

- Daily exercise for a minimum of thirty minutes. It could be anything from working out at the gym to a brisk walk. Get your blood pumping!
- Just as it's essential to move, it's important to stop. Develop the habit of meditating every day for at least thirty minutes. Learn to clean up your head from all the distractions that may cloud your thinking.
- Make time for your friends and family. (No, sending a funny GIF in the family group chat doesn't count!) Try going out for lunch, camping, hiking, going to an adventure park, or playing board games—as long as you spend good, old-fashioned, organic time with them!
- Learn a new skill! This pandemic has been immensely valuable for pushing people into doing this! Locked up in their homes with nothing else to do, many of the sparingly used ovens found newfound purpose when myriad people discovered a love for baking! If that's not your forte, there are literally millions of things you can choose from—all a click away on the internet!

Whatever the case is for you, if you don't know what to do, doing nothing won't help your case. You cannot wait for clarity to enter your life out of nowhere; you need to welcome and embrace it. A good start is determining your authentic values and then creating the goals that are aligned with what is most important to you. Here is a table with a simple exercise you can do:

What is important to me in my inner world?	What is important to me in my outer world?	What goal do I need to set to harmonize those two worlds?
My well-being	My physical appearance	Meditate daily for twenty minutes. Exercise daily for forty-five minutes.
Security, feeling safe, not worrying about money.	Get a better job, ask for a promotion, seek new ways to get more clients, grow my income, be financially independent.	Apply for new jobs, invest in AI to get more clients booked, hire a coach to help you build wealth faster.

Before moving on to the next section, open a Word document or use a pen and paper to complete this exercise to create goals and associate action in alliance with your authentic values.

Breaking the Chains of Ambiguity

One of the most concerning dilemmas that stem from lacking clarity is ambiguity. Ambiguity means to lack exactness, something that can be interpreted in more than one way. Opacity is excellent if you're a writer or a director. Having elements of ambiguity in works of art suggests a deeper meaning. However, in everyday life, ambiguity can lead to a loss of cohesion between people and a lack of comprehension.

Ambiguity stems from a lack of clarity. To fully reap the rewards of this chapter's teachings, it is essential to learn how to handle ambiguity.

Practice Mindfulness

Lack of clarity causes ambiguity, but while you worry about what's to come, you miss out on today. The first step in eliminating ambiguity is to appreciate the beauty of the here and now. For that, you need to practice mindfulness: being present and experiencing the moment to the fullest. By focusing your mind on the task at hand, you gain a degree of clarity. Your mind focuses on what's in front of it rather than worrying about what's to come.

Avoid Speculation

Humans have a terrible habit of predicting the future for a particular set of events—and then believing it. You cannot possibly predict the exact future, but you can plan for it today. Make good decisions and plan out your actions to change the trajectory of your life. Keep in mind that nothing is set in stone; you can plan whatever you want, but you will only obtain what you're destined for. John. F. Kennedy said, "Change is the law of life. Those who only look to the past or the present are certain to miss the future."

Be Confident

A significant part of dealing with uncertainty and ambiguity is building the confidence to handle things that aren't in your control. Stay true to your authentic values. Believe in your beliefs. It's okay to be wrong sometimes—as long as you learn from your mistakes. By implementing these qualities into your daily life, you will respond and adapt more successfully.

Embrace Change

Embracing change helps eliminate ambiguity by clarifying your responses and adding new beliefs and viewpoints to something that never existed before. Keep an open mind and fine-tune the course of action you plan to take—just how an archer hits the bull's eye!

Make Informed Decisions

If you overthink things—like I do—you know how arduous decision-making can be. Ambiguity can mean that you don't necessarily make the correct decision, but don't let that stop you. A wrong decision can be better than no decision. If you dared to do something for yourself, be proud! Invest the energy, money, and time needed to get the clarity you need to make those crucial decisions. Make sure that whatever decision you make is in alignment with what you value the most in life. That's progress. Remember that a mistake is just an opportunity to learn!

Learn to Accept

In life, you will encounter many situations where you simply do not know what is happening or what will happen. It is imperative that you embrace things as they are—with a newfound sense of clarity—and learn to engage with things as they present themselves.

The only thing sure about life is that it is uncertain. If life were predictable, wouldn't that be boring? We can't predict how things will turn out, but we can try our best to plan for the future. The COVID-19 pandemic is a perfect example of this. No one assumed it would alter the course of humanity in a matter of months, causing the world to adjust a "new normal."

Now that you understand the concept of clarity and its relation to ambiguity, let's take an in-depth look at how it can be implemented with this chapter's principle.

A simple way to remember the first principle is to keep these three words in mind: what, why, and when.

"What you want" extends far beyond the physical realm. From earthly needs, wanting a relationship, a family, a new job, a car, or maybe a house, to spiritual needs, having your chakras opened, being at peace with yourself, or finding the deeper meaning of who you indeed are, it's all up to you.

"Why you want" follows suit. You could want a new relationship or a job because you feel limited at your current one, a new car because yours has done its time and it's time for an upgrade, or the new house because it's time you paid money toward a mortgage on something you owned rather than renting. Similarly, having your chakras opened can help you attain unforeseen levels of calmness and content.

"When you want" depends entirely on you and what you feel would be the correct course of action. You could want a new job as soon as possible. A raise would allow you to get a new car, and by saving money over time, you could eventually buy a new house for yourself. You choose the priority of how things want to go, planning out things according to your life. You might want mental peace above everything else! Keep in mind that anything is possible to achieve if you set your mind to it. Remember principle 1: "To break free from ambiguity, clarify what you want, why you want it, and when you want it."

5

FINE-TUNE YOUR VISION OF EXCELLENCE

Principle 2: Awakening your astronomical vision requires committing to something bigger than yourself.

Dreaming is an integral part of the human psyche. We start having dreams right in infancy, and we don't stop until we die. You dream every single night, but you forget a majority of your dreams when you wake up. However, there are still quite a few you can remember. In fact, there might be some dreams you've remembered for years. Apart from humans, a significant portion of animals also dream. Your cat or dog might be having a wonderful dream of seeing their food bowl filled to the brim—or a nightmare of being chased by a vacuum cleaner! Whatever the case may be, one thing differentiates our dreams from animals: we can make them a reality.

All of us dream about being successful in life and being content with our careers, families, partners, and so on. Yet, most of the time, it stays just that: a dream. The turning point in making dreams a reality is having a vision of excellence. What does it mean to have a vision of excellence? This vision requires a clear and concise sense of purpose and understanding. We ought to have a much holistic view of every aspect of our lives. Instead of picking momentary, short-term goals that handle events one at a time, we learn to focus on the bigger picture. This vision that goes beyond our egoistical needs and serves a more significant number of people.

Visions are derived from our authentic values, and our values emerge as solutions to the voids we feel or create as a result of wanting to turn our dreams into reality. Establishing a vision for life provides us with a direction to move: forward. Having a clear vision is crucial if you wish to realize your goals and unlock your greatest potential. If reaching your goals means climbing to the top of the ladder of success, having a vision entails all of that ladder's steps. Creating a values-driven vision of excellence helps put meaning behind your goals. It helps you maintain your focus to keep you working hard even when the going gets tough.

It's also worth mentioning that your definition of success might be quite different from anyone else's definition. As long as you remain steadfast in making your visions a reality, nothing can faze you. When you know what you want to accomplish in life, you will see evidence in your existence if you've gotten closer to a fulfilled life. By knowing what success means to you, you can be confident in the decisions you make.

Elon Musk and Greta Thunberg are both visionaries in their own right, but they have wildly different prospects. Elon has envisioned humans colonizing Mars within the next century, and Greta fights for climate change and safeguarding our planet. American TV sensation Oprah Winfrey and British business magnate Richard Branson are wildly successful entrepreneurs with different visions and goals. These are just a handful of examples of immensely successful visionaries who paved the way for millions of others to prosper by becoming living examples of the very things they preach. All of them figured out their life's calling and dedicated themselves to achieving it.

Here are a few steps for finding a vision for your life:

List the steps. It doesn't matter how far down the line your dreams and goals are; you need to write down detailed steps you need to take to turn your visions into reality. At the very least, make a rough outline with all the steps you need to take, the possible hurdles you could encounter, and how you plan to solve them should the time come.

- Write a vision statement for yourself. This might seem like something you would find in companies, but it is just as crucial for you! Often, your vision statement consists of all of the goals you plan to achieve, what matters to you the most, and how you aim to improve yourself and others around you.
- Be bold. Let your vision take you above and beyond what you aim to do. It may sound outlandish, feel inspiring, and push you to work hard enough to make it a reality. If you follow the flock, don't expect to make a difference!
- Outline your beliefs. Now that you have defined your vision of excellence, let's see if what you believe matches the mental picture you want for your life. If not, what steps can you take to change them to create beliefs that match the destiny you want for yourself. We could all benefit from a little more self-belief in our lives. As children, you may have been told to believe in yourself, but many of you feel that no one ever seemed to be able to explain how until now.

The fantastic combination of belief, expectation, and intent is one of the world's best-kept secrets. When combined, they become an unstoppable force, enabling people's lives to be transformed in ways they hadn't previously dared to imagine.

The power of belief and positive expectation will transform your life, the lives of your children, and even your company's fortunes.

The call to a completely different life awaits you within the pages of this book. Will you act on that call?

It is up to you to use what you are learning to harness the power of belief and expectation and create powerful, self-fulfilling prophecies, to help your children make empowering beliefs during the imprint period, and understand how transforming your thoughts can improve your health, rewrite your future, and end procrastination forever.

So, what do you believe in? Is what you believe limiting you or helping you climb to greater heights? What beliefs will get you where you want to get to? What are the things in the world that you want to be changed? What things that you wish to remain the same? Ensure that your beliefs and what you value the most in life coincide with the vision of excellence you want. Achieving harmony between voids, values, beliefs, and behaviors is essential for manifesting your vision of excellence. Keep evolving it as you go through the eight cycles of life; it will serve as a compass that will keep you on your path to achieving excellence in whatever you set your mind to.

Your calling in life might not come at a fixed time. Colonel Sanders, the man behind the global fast-food chain, was nearly sixty years old when KFC began to get the notoriety it deserved! Daniel Radcliffe was only eleven years old when he starred in the first Harry Potter movie, which ultimately led to more than a decade of acting, making him one of the highest-paid child actors of the time! These are two extremes of when a person can find their calling. Remember that you won't magically figure out what you want to do in life when you graduate from high school, college, or university.

Establishing what has inspired you in pivotal moments in your past and present can help you clarify the vision of excellence for your future. When I look back at all the things that happened in my life, the good and the bad, particular deeper callings have always been there with me. I always loved learning, finding solutions to life's problems, and using what I learned to make others feel good about themselves and improve the quality of their lives and businesses.

I have always loved traveling, exploring, and learning about new scientific discoveries, cultures, civilizations, and ways of thinking, living, and being. I have always dreamed of creating a life manual for people to refer to when they needed to fix, improve, or change something in their lives—just like the manuals that come with pretty much every product we buy.

I care about animals, nature, justice, human rights, and equality and equal opportunities. I love learning about business, building wealth, writing, managing people, customer service, and cooking. My entrepreneurial parents owned a family restaurant in Zenica, Bosnia and Herzegovina. We produced most of the restaurant's food on our farm in what is now known as the Republic of North Macedonia.

I can provide multiple examples that establish the voids that instinctively drive what you value in life. That ultimately determines your ever-evolving mission and vision of excellence in life.

In 2009, having faced the challenges, fears, and uncertainty that came with being made redundant from a job I truly loved and invested more than nine years into, I sat down to clarify my authentic values and vision of excellence. To inspire your creative juices, here is what I wrote:

> I, Tony Jeton Selimi, declare before myself, others, and God, that my primary mission and vision of excellence in life is to travel the world inspiring and teaching men and women of all professions, nationalities, creeds, and colors to become purposeful and disciplined masters of themselves and dedicated and inspired leaders and teachers of others. I do so by speaking, consulting, writing the world's best books, creating inspired films and documentaries, and sharing insights, lessons, and one-of-a-kind methods. Globally, I coach, mentor, and train people from all professions and

businesses from all market sectors to build spiritual, mental, emotional, physical, vocational/business, financial, familial, and social awareness. We can serve humanity more effectively and efficiently and consciously direct human consciousness evolution by exemplifying high human potential.

My unshakeable purpose in life is to help one billion people grow into their fullest potential and achieve their vision of excellence, which has become faster and more accessible due to the advent of technology. To infiltrate and use my one-of-a-kind, science-driven, and experienced proven methods and teachings to grow, empower, and transform business, leadership, government, health care, education, and current and future ambitions to conquer space. Ultimately, contribute to accomplishing the seventeen UN development goals and keep solving the growing humankind problems as we venture in the terra incognita.

This ever-evolving vision of excellence I set in 2009 has lifted me up every time I was pushed down by my disempowered transient personas or others' judgments and opinions of me. Frequently clarifying and updating my vision of excellence has given me hope each time I feel hopeless. It has inspired me to keep going forward and expand my frontiers of what is possible.

Determine Your Life's Calling

It might seem like a daunting task at first, but the universe has already been providing you with ample opportunities to find and fulfill your calling in life. All you need to do is pay attention.

By paying attention to the people you interact with, the types of things you notice, the specific kinds of locales that draw you in, the books you read, and even the kind of dreams you have, you can see how the universe is helping you on your path to excellence. The guide laid down by the cosmos is just an indication of your earthly goals and missions. Make a habit of writing down as many of your dreams and inspirational moments as you can. Also, make sure you identify which of your core values the experiences, people, and places you are attracted to help you fulfill.

Another equally important facet of finding your life's purpose is the ability to utilize creative expression. A significant majority of us might not have an artistic background or simply have enough time to partake in any creative activities. Even if you get the chance for a few minutes a day, do something creative. Use Canva to squeeze out your creative juices, doodle, sketch, sing, or dance. This is an excellent way to destress and get your mind off things, and it creates more neural pathways in your brain to facilitate creative thinking and allow you to think outside the box more freely.

Perhaps the best way to reignite creativity that has been dulled down by life is to take a trip down memory lane. Go through old photographs of you as a child and try to remember all the hopes and aspirations you had back then. Figure out whether those things would bring you joy now and whether you can partake in them again. You will notice what feels good and what doesn't—make a note of it every time you do. Slowly cut down on distractions that waste your time. An hour spent mindlessly scrolling on social media or watching TV is a wasted hour of your life that could have been better utilized on yourself. Cut the habit of distractions, learn to live in the moment, and value the people and places around you.

A lot of us have to post whatever we do online. The "likes" we receive are part of a positive feedback loop. Our ancient ancestors lived in tribes of no more than fifteen or twenty people, and getting "tribal approval" is part of our DNA. This was never designed for hundreds or thousands or millions of people online, and it's easy to get addicted. Learn to break the cycle and focus on tangible things that can equate to happiness, fulfillment, and love.

When looking for your life's purpose, never shy away from experiencing new things—whether it's exotic cuisine or doing something entirely out of character for you, like square dancing! It will be a memorable experience, and you might find something that you love.

Finally, be patient. Discovering your path in life isn't something that will magically happen overnight. You need to be patient and mindful with yourself during the process. This whole procedure will take a lot of intention and effort; after all, you are figuring out your calling in life! It is worth every minute.

Overcoming Obstacles: Learning the Key to Being Content with Yourself

You might have had dreams about your life, but time and time again, they felt nearly impossible to accomplish. Even if you've written down your vision and have a set idea for how you would go about determining your life's calling, your dreams always seem an arm's length away. We often lose focus on our dreams because we get tangled in a net of obstacles. Let's figure out how these obstacles arise and how you can stop them.

Stop Comparing Yourself to Other People

There's a fine line between appreciating someone for their accomplishments and comparing yourself to them. If you look up to Elon Musk as a wildly successful entrepreneur and learn from him, that's great! However, if you look at him and think, *Wow, I will be the next Musk,* then you're comparing yourself to him. Retain your originality; you are authentically "unfakeable."

You can be inspired by people, but it does not equate to wanting to be them and losing yourself in the process. A lot of underlying factors helped people achieve their goals, given their circumstances. No person will have the same life experiences, style, and knowledge. Ultimately, you are living your authentic life. Focus on developing yourself. You are a continuous work in progress and not a static entity. The only person you can compare yourself to is your past. Did you improve yourself from how you were before? Did you improve your behavior? Did you achieve something significant?

Practicing Perfectionism

If you delay making decisions by waiting for the "right" chance, you miss out on opportunities to grow and better yourself. There will be decisions that need careful planning, like buying a house or a car, but confident choices could benefit you in the long run, such as quitting your toxic job for another one that pays less but is much more manageable. There is nothing worth more than your health and peace of mind—and that's why you work so hard! If things do not proceed as planned, know that most decisions are reversible.

Stop Caring about What Others Think

Ultimately, you are living your life, and they are living theirs. If someone doesn't like the way you are as a person—or minor details such as the way you dress, look, who you love, what you stand for—it's a shining example of how flawed they are as a person. They need help.

When people lack certain qualities in themselves, they nitpick others. However, this doesn't mean you close yourself off to every opinion. Constructive criticism with valuable insight from family, friends, coaches, employers, and colleagues is always helpful for improving yourself. It's easy to look out for this in a snide remark!

Rejection is just another person's opinion. It tells you what that person thinks, but it says nothing about you as an individual, the hardships you have endured, and the road you have trekked to be the individual you are today.

Reject the Fear of Failure

Fear is an innate behavioral trait that is present in all living things. It's beneficial for animals and helps them avoid danger. Most people and animals share a fear of loud sounds, heights, and the dark. Our brains keep us safe and out of danger by scanning our environments and deciding what can and cannot harm us. The problem with us is that this transcends far beyond the average "fear of heights." We begin to speculate and imagine things going wrong by focusing on the most detrimental outcome of any decision we make. Instead of letting fear grip you, try to analyze it critically. If you're afraid of losing your job, why? What draws you so much to your employment? Are there no other options available to you? Every failure is a lesson to learn from. The road to excellence is riddled with failures you will encounter, but it's about dusting yourself off and getting back to it.

There will be many obstacles on the path to accomplishing a worthwhile goal. When those obstacles appear, it's easy to lose your belief and the motivation to continue on the same path.

Most of us have a general goal and a direction: to live a healthy life, have a happy family, and provide for them and ourselves to the best of our ability. Ultimately, we want to enjoy life. Some of us have a little motivation because we're trying something, but that isn't enough.

To succeed in life, you need to do more than try things. Completely changing gears every time there's an obstacle will get you nowhere. You need to make an absolute commitment to the process and push through the countless roadblocks you encounter along the way. It is a process of committing to a vision of excellence and the path that will take you there by taking action, noticing your results, and then making gradual shifts in your approach until the results start to show up in your external reality.

How can you tell if you lack commitment? Just listen to the language you use when you talk to yourself and other people about why you do what you do, who you are doing it for, and how you do it. I happen to have a perfect example.

Below are some excerpts from an email I received a few weeks ago from someone "interested" in the Vital Planning for Elevated Living program. Put the quotes in context. The email states that he has taken "a lot" of personal development training:

- "To be honest … consistent results have eluded me … make some … lose some"
- "Five days of intense coaching is hard to digest … I lack the motivation required."
- "What I am looking for is a free consultation to try, and then maybe I will buy the coaching package … I want to try a session, and if I like it, I will pay you for it."

Talk about lack of commitment! No wonder results have eluded him. No one gets substantial long-term results when they lack commitment toward a vision of excellence. It's like the laws of nature and trying to defy the law of gravity. I have never heard of any restaurant or grocery store letting you try their food for a month and then asking if you will pay for future purchases. Be cautious not to give in to this disempowered way of thinking. Many of my clients who book a clarity coaching consultation know the value of one session or the benefits of a five-day advanced coaching and training session.

If you are a coach, consultant, trainer, or therapist, be wary of people who devalue your service and want to waste your most precious asset: your time. Imagine what would happen to your business if ten thousand people booked a free consultation with you so they could try your services. You would end up frustrated, drained, and demotivated. It is wise to remain in fair exchange. Instead, focus your time on clients who are serious about working with you to solve a problem that causes them headaches or pain and are committed to climbing to greater heights.

As the value and service I provide to my clients grew, the kind of clients I started to coach and mentor changed. I began to attract clients who valued my expertise and knowledge and put all their resources into creating the kind of future they envisioned for themselves, their loved ones, and their business: mental, emotional, and financial energy and time.

I feel for those who may have this approach. I used to have it when my circumstances stopped me from truly going for what I wanted. When I see something like this, I can relate to it because I know this person is experiencing a problem or pain that blinds them from creating abundance. A lack of belief in their infinite abilities to make what they want stops many people from using a proportion of their income for self-mastery and hiring an experienced and qualified coach who can help them achieve results faster. When I have spoken on various topics, I meet people who spend money on unnecessary luxury items, hoping they will stumble across an easy way to make money, heal their pain, and feel fulfilled. Good luck with that!

Zig Ziglar said, "Most people who fail in their dreams fail not from lack of ability but lack of commitment."

Here is an idea worth adopting and sharing: Just as you need oxygen for life, when the going gets tough, the authentic genius inside you needs a clear vision of excellence to focus upon. Before you move on to the next chapter, here is an exercise for you to do:

1. Identify your fears, blockages, values, and voids.
2. Know the difference between your injected and authentic values.

3. Make a list of high-priority values and use them to write down a bold and detailed vision of excellence.
4. Pinpoint the kind of beliefs you need to adopt to achieve the vision you just wrote.
5. List specific action steps that you will commit to taking daily.

Each time you are ready to take another challenge, create another breakthrough, and achieve bigger things in life, make sure you use principle 2: "Awakening your astronomical vision requires committing to something bigger than yourself."

6

AVOIDING CHALLENGES IS FUTILE; FACING THEM IS COURAGEOUS

Principle 3: To build your resilience, it is wise to immediately confront any issues that arise and respond mindfully and objectively.

Practicing mindfulness is a theme that you will see throughout this book because it often holds a significant degree of importance. The third principle discusses how to be more resilient in life and effectively deal with issues or problems in your life that you keep avoiding.

There are several problems we all face daily. Getting a flat tire is a problem—as is binge eating or getting reprimanded at work. Naturally, each situation has its own "gravity." You cannot compare a flat tire, which is an inconvenience at best, to something like binge eating, which adversely affects your physical health—and is often due to poor emotional or mental health.

People are struggling all around the world. The struggle is an undeniable part of all living things—from the tiny seeds in the ground that struggle to break through to the surface to the single parent working two jobs to ensure their children's ends are met.

Struggles are of varying sizes and intensities, but they all have one thing in common: they improve you. To survive, a seed in the ground will try to break apart a boulder that weighs several tons. The single parent would efficiently work more than fifty hours a week and still make sure their child is well fed and has the best toys or books.

Obstacles serve a much more significant role other than perceived emotional "distress." By learning how to face challenges, you can power on through more significant problems when they arise. You will know how to leave behind ideologies that do not result in results. We have all undergone hardships on a near-daily basis. Everyone reacts to obstacles in a different way, some better than others, but it's worth remembering that the choices you make are yours alone. It may not be an easy choice to make; no one wants to face their problems when they can just avoid them.

Obstacles diverge your life into two paths. The easy road is where you simply ignore your problems or do a botched fix for them. Most people tend to take this route since it's smooth sailing. On the other hand, facing challenges and resolving them is the road less traveled. Like pulling off a Band-Aid, it will sting for a bit, but it will ultimately benefit you. Let's discuss just how vital obstacles are for your growth.

The Importance of Encountering Obstacles

Obstacles serve a pivotal role in helping you shape your unfakeable identity. There will be multiple instances in your life where the challenges you face will take an emotional, physical, and financial toll on you. Obstacles serve as a way for you to go further than your learned limits. All of this is only possible once you acknowledge what obstacles you face, rank them from the smallest to the largest, and list at least one hundred disadvantages and benefits. When you clarify all the specific problems and identify the pains and pleasures, you begin to actively and objectively face them.

The obstacles in your life will either derail you from being on course toward achieving your goals or direct the actions you take so you are a step closer to excellence. Try to identify practices, habits, places, or even people that cause you discomfort or raise obstacles for you. Keep in mind that every obstacle you encounter has a solution. However, if you can actively avoid a problem altogether, shouldn't you?

You can avoid only a finite number of obstacles because blocks are practically infinite! No one is born ready to withstand challenges. It's something we all learn from the school of hard knocks. Just as the newborn gazelle needs to learn how to walk and run within minutes of being born or get eaten, we have our problems (albeit on a wider scale). As long as you are alive, you will continuously overcome ever-surmounting difficulties. Would you prefer to be stuck in a rut forever?

An easier way to manage obstacles is to focus on the bigger picture—the light at the end of the tunnel, the end in mind. When you concentrate your energy and attention toward the "bigger picture," every other obstacle loses significance and becomes an "inconvenience" at best. Naturally, if you don't have a fixed goal to attune your mind to, every block, no matter how insignificant, will impose itself as a significant concern. Keeping laser precision on your goals will ensure that the issues cause you no problems.

Most importantly, learn to embrace obstacles objectively! When you're pushed against a wall, your creativity and ingenuity are at their peaks. It takes endless persistence and resistance to fully overcome obstacles, which can be achieved only when there are seemingly no other options.

Most of our modern-day technological marvels were made solely due to the fact that people were pushed against a wall. NASA and Elon Musk have developed space travel, which had its foundations laid during World War II. Nazi Germany, in a futile effort to win a losing war, developed the first missiles ever created, which ultimately served as the blueprint for rockets and aircraft for decades to come. This technological breakthrough ultimately helped send a man to the moon in 1969. Coincidentally, it is also the year I was born. How cool is that?

Similarly, obstacles create blueprints for a better version of you. Since your perception of life is determined by your outcome, it is only apparent that a life shaped by overcoming obstacles would be remarkable. In some instances, you will see how obstacles genuinely help you discover meaning in your life. Perhaps you face an obstacle, and you solve it, only to realize how good you are at solving said obstacle! The obstacle could have been while building a business or caring for a sick animal. Every person possesses an innate potential for things, which can only be accessed if presented with a situation.

Overcoming Obstacles

Facing obstacles is the first step. The next step is understanding how to overcome them. The first thing in this process is finding out what limits us. Certain limiting factors prevent us from achieving simple goals. For example, if you can't meet deadlines at work or school, and your excuse is "I don't have enough time," then you are simply creating obstacles for yourself. Everyone has the same twenty-four hours in a day; they are just managed differently. An unproductive hour spent scrolling through social media could be utilized elsewhere. Instead of sleeping until noon, waking up early cab set a precedent for a better work ethic.

It is worth noticing how long you have dealt with a given obstacle. We often drag things out much longer than they need to be by getting distracted. The only surefire way to know this is to think of the last obstacle you have overcome and how long it took to overcome it. Obstacles usually require incremental steps to overcome them. It doesn't take one leap to get on top of a mountain; there are thousands of steps along the way. It is much easier and more manageable to divide your obstacles and treat them one at a time. This is made possible by maintaining an active plan to do so. Write down everything that counts as an obstacle. Regardless of how good you think your memory is, it's always better to write things down. A simple list of pros and cons is an effective and objective way of dealing with them for applicable obstacles. Prioritize them in alignment with what is most important to you in that specific moment and reach for excellence. Don't forget to write about how you overcame them—and never forget to reward yourself for doing so!

Finally, it is wise to come to terms with the fact that you cannot solve every problem. Many things are going to be out of your control. This is where you learn how to adapt, delegate, and improvise to overcome obstacles rather than staying hung up on them.

Incorporating the Octagon of Excellence's Transitional Cycles to Overcome Obstacles

Transition

Learn to break down your obstacles into smaller, more manageable segments. For example, if you have trouble managing time, write down how you spend your time throughout the day and see where you can make adjustments. Reducing a mere twenty minutes from a Netflix binge could do wonders for your sleep and your schedule!

Regeneration

Every obstacle you overcome makes you a better version of yourself. Just as you "level up" in video games, you do this in life, You get regenerated into a better you—someone who is more capable of overcoming obstacles and finding your path.

Focus

When you turn your attention toward actively engaging with your obstacles rather than avoiding them, you exponentially improve your focus and understanding in the process. You become more capable of reading through situations, allowing you to analyze things far better than before. It is where focus grows that the energy flows.

Rebirth

Like regeneration, major obstacles and hurdles in life can cause a systemic rebirth to your very being. Overcoming the loss of a loved one is a prime example of this. You get over your grief, but the very essence of that person becomes a part of your being. You get rebirthed into a new version of yourself. The same happens when you go from one job to another, one relationship to another, or one business idea to another. Each time you are ready to transcend to higher levels of awareness, you destroy what no longer serves you—and you give birth to something that helps you get through the next steps of your never-ending journey through life.

Balance

Empowering every critical area of life is essential for maintaining a healthy balance. On this self-empowerment journey, you will need to face many obstacles. The more obstacles you actively engage in, the easier it is to bring balance to your life. No one thing in particular bogs you down, and you can maintain a perfect balance with everything in your life. It is also easier to take your life to a whole new level when you face every challenge head-on.

Service

You can only truly help others once you know how to help yourself. By being of service to yourself, you, in turn, can be of service to others. You do that by filling the most significant voids and their corresponding values. The more you do this, the more you build the knowledge, skills, and tools to solve critical problems. When you solve significant issues, your service to humankind will become even more excellent.

Unity

A lot of problem-solving is a collective effort. There will be obstacles in your life that you and your partner, family, friends, or colleagues will need to come together to resolve. Every significant breakthrough that humanity has achieved occurred because of a collective effort. The same applies to ensuring that your children get the best education, your team achieves its sales targets, or your company keeps being a market leader. Whether you are a loving partner, husband, mother, friend, busy professional, or company leader, whatever you have achieved resulted from a collective effort. Resolving obstacles provides closure and provides unity for you and the other people.

Infinity

The concept of infinity is most prominent here. If we want to reach for excellence in a chosen field, role, or job, it is wise to look into what the concept of infinity teaches us. Since obstacles start from the moment you take your first breath, they will evolve, grow, and change until the moment you take your last breath. Drawing knowledge, strength, and insights from the infinity of our nature enforces the fact that life provides a series of obstacles, and overcoming them puts you on the road to self-actualization.

So, before you move on to the next chapter, remember principle 3: "To build your resilience, it is wise to immediately confront any issues that arise and respond mindfully and objectively."

7

STOP WHEN SOMETHING DOES NOT FEEL RIGHT OR LOOK RIGHT

Principle 4: Making mistakes is human; correcting them awakens your excellence.

Mistakes play an integral part in the development of every human being. Mistakes help you develop your ability to choose wisely between right from wrong and offer an opportunity for growth from those mistakes if you choose to accept it.

Growing up, we are never taught the importance of making mistakes. Instead, most of us are reprimanded for making them in the first place. I'm sure you have numerous recollections of making mistakes as a child, which you were scolded for. This hard-wires your brain to stop making mistakes rather than allowing you the opportunity to learn from what went wrong. Being raised this way embeds fear into your subconscious; something as mundane as breaking a plate or a glass might trigger anxiety.

Naturally, this becomes a slippery slope that follows us well into adulthood. People begin to hide their mistakes, despite knowing they're in the wrong. At work or school, the fear of getting reprimanded becomes so intense that people choose to ignore their blunders and build upon them instead. When we ignore our mistakes, we never come to terms with them. It's the equivalent of a cardiologist refusing to look at the EKG report and simply prescribing medicine on a whim, ultimately resulting in the patient's death—and the doctor's medical license being revoked.

There are ample examples of people who turn their lives around from the point of no return. We see countless stories of ex-convicts who learn from their mistakes and turn their lives around. Robert Downey Jr. is one such example. From being addicted to cocaine and other drugs, and ultimately getting arrested for it in the 1990s and early 2000s, he turned his life around. He focused on his failing acting career and took on the notorious role of Iron Man, becoming part of Marvel's billion-dollar franchise.

What Mistakes Offer Us

It's hard to conceptualize the fact that mistakes inevitably do equal good and harm, irrespective of whether you're the one on the receiving end of someone's mistake or the person making a mistake. Being on the receiving end allows us to guide those who falter. There is no better sign of maturity and growth than a person who readily accepts their mistakes, and the reverse is true as well. Before we can proceed, it's crucial to understand how to turn mistakes into lessons that support your quest for excellence:

Step 1: Acknowledgment

The first—and often the hardest—part of making a mistake is acknowledging it. It's wise to wholeheartedly admit to where you were wrong rather than playing the blame game with others. Pretending mistakes never happened or downplaying what you did only helps you lie to yourself, which doesn't work.

Step 2: Claim 100 Percent Responsibility

This is easier said than done. It is fundamental to claim your responsibility and take necessary action in accordance with it. This might mean apologizing to someone or going out of your way to fix your mistake. It is a sign of maturity to do so.

When you think about it, no one truly wants to have more responsibility. Instead, I teach my clients to transition from feeling they have to take responsibility into an awareness that acknowledges their "response-ability." A slight mental shift like this can help you take 100 percent ownership of your life and significantly impact your journey to growing into your potential.

Step 3: Be Specific

Being specific requires finding the root cause of your mistake. It is wise to go through the five Ws: who, what, where, when, and why. Doing so will give you greater clarity and confidence.

Step 4: Plan Out Your Next Mode of Action

On your journey to correct a mistake, make a list of all the steps needed. The best plans have more than one option for fixing the issues, granting you multiple ways to do so.

Step 5: Remain Flexible To Your Plan

Correcting your mistakes may require constant supervision. Your final plan may differ significantly from the plan you initially thought of. It is necessary to keep an open mind and be ready and willing to change.

Now that we know how to turn mistakes into lessons and strengths, let's look at how they help us:

Mistakes offer us a sense of clarity.

A misdirection we learn in our early lives is that mistakes mean we have messed up somehow, and we ought to suffer the consequences. However, identifying the actions and outcomes that prevented us from reaching our desired outcome offers us immense clarity about why we were stopped. Mistakes provide an opportunity to gauge why we diverted from our initial goals and help put us on the right track.

Mistakes help us face our fears.

Mistakes help us admit where we were wrong and allow us to make tangible progress in correcting them. Facing our fears grants us the necessary clarity, power, and resilience to grow from our mistakes.

Mistakes foster a sense of courage.

It takes courage to admit to your mistakes, and it helps our emotional maturity grow. Growing our courage will help us become better leaders, better partners, and better human beings.

Mistakes help us be creative:

Oftentimes, when we are stuck in a rut, it is due to a mistake. When we are pushed up against a wall, we learn to find alternative routes to overcome our mistakes. We reconsider our priorities and adjust our actions to handle our newfound mode of action.

Stop when something does not feel right.

Frequently, the best way to correct your mistakes is to learn from previous patterns and avoid them altogether. Recall the moments when something just didn't feel right. That is the universe's way of telling you to avoid a problem. You may get this feeling while meeting a person, doing your job, or contemplating going outside. Learn to trust your gut. Why did such feelings develop in the first place? Research and analyze the events and circumstances that led to this. Encouraging yourself, your partner, your children, your employees, your clients, and your young leaders to notice errors and fix them is the first step in creating accountability and independence and putting them on a path to excellence.

To be independent, stop and notice your errors.

Make it known to yourself that stopping and noticing a mistake is very important and something that you can celebrate. It requires paying attention to meaning and visual information and is a strategy you need to become independent.

Take a moment to congratulate yourself for being so committed, determined, and focused on your journey to transcend low-level thinking so you can grow your potential and be more of who you know you are. Let's utilize the Octagon of Excellence's Eight Cs: clarify, commit, confront, correct, consult, collaborate, compliment, and celebrate to stop, identify errors, fix them, learn the lessons, and remain on track to excellence.

Clarify

Acknowledging and accepting your mistakes helps clarify your next steps and prevents the errors from muddying your thinking process. You have already put yourself on the path to correction and granted yourself exceptional clarity, which helps your future decisions remain fruitful to your growth.

Commit

Mistakes allow you to commit to improving yourself. You know you messed up, and you know the only way to move forward is to improve yourself. Hence, to grow as a person and reach your most tremendous potential, it is necessary to commit to self-improvement.

Confront

Confronting your mistakes grants you the indomitable strength to question yourself. It helps you realize that no one is immune to making mistakes—no matter how great the person is. Everyone is susceptible to making mistakes, and that's okay.

Correct

Once you know where you're wrong, you can see where to fix it. A mistake can be nothing more than a learning experience, and correcting it grants you that.

Consult

Perhaps you cannot decipher the reason for your mistake. In that case, it is necessary to consult with a professional and someone with more experience. It is admirable, courageous, and wise to know when you're wrong and to know when to seek help from those who know better. Many of my global clients have reached out to me to help them clarify, decipher, and plan the steps that prevent repeated mistakes.

Collaborate

In your journey to correct yourself, you may very well encounter people who have made the same mistakes as you. This is especially common in relationships, friendships, careers, and workspaces. It is necessary to collaborate with them and mutually improve yourself, making it easier for everyone.

Compliments

Working on your mistakes is an admirable task, and your progress deserves compliments. It is a gradual progress that takes time, but praising and acknowledging your path to correction plays a crucial role in your journey to excellence.

Celebrate

Lastly, don't forget to celebrate your progress! Every time you learn from your mistakes and move forward with your life, you create a new version of yourself, which calls for a celebration. You only get a step closer to excellence every time you do so.

In summary, it is wise to instruct your mind to see mistakes as lessons and opportunities for growth. Next time you tell yourself you've made a mistake, remember principle 4: Making mistakes is human; correcting them awakens your excellence.

8

BRIDGE THE GAP BETWEEN YOUR CURRENT LIFE AND YOUR DESIRED LIFE

Principle 5: For better, more efficient, and more effective results, seek expert advice.

The implications of instant gratification have caused near-irreparable damage to our society. We have all been so numbed down by what we see on social media that we consider ourselves failures if we cannot follow suit. You will see influencers and wealthy content creators living luxurious lifestyles while implying that you have wasted your life if you cannot achieve all of what they've done.

I like to refer to this as the "short-term gain, long-term pain" mindset. The hedonistic lifestyle a lot of people have adopted looks excellent for the time being. They spend most of their income financing their exuberant lifestyles and have little to no worthwhile investments. If you look back thirty or forty years, people were content with whatever they had when social media did not exist. There was a higher emphasis on having a fruitful career or occupation than on instant gratification. The result? More people were content with their lives than they are today. They had jobs that financed their lives for decades, and they could save up enough money to invest later.

We ought to be happier today than previous generations were. We have TVs, reliable cars, which were only beginning to gain popularity one hundred years ago, access to clean water and food, and the ability to communicate with anyone around the world in less than a second. Despite all of this, many people think, *If I had all the stuff I wanted, I would be happy.*

Many people have made "getting what they want" the source of their happiness. Some multimillionaires have everything they can buy, but they are not content with their lives. The sheer concept of happiness is much more than getting what you want; it involves a paradigm shift.

This is where the hedonic treadmill comes into play. In a nutshell, this theory shows how all humans tend to return to a baseline level of happiness, irrespective of what events, positive or negative, occur in their lives. A more holistic look into this theory comes from looking at society. There have been rapid advancements in every single aspect of our lives. Our lives have become much more straightforward than the lives of our ancestors—even just one hundred years ago.

After a while, we get accustomed to the technology we have. We can all relate to when smartphones became a thing, from clunky Nokia phones and Blackberries to the first iPhone. We are so used to them today that we know there will be a new phone released every year. This pattern continues in our personal lives as well. Many of us run on this hedonic treadmill like a hamster wheel, working until we can afford something we want to buy, feeling brief satisfaction from it, and then finding something else to continue the cycle.

A lot of people falsely assume that buying the latest phone, the newest car, or the most expensive designer clothes will make them feel better. This is *affective forecasting*. Unfortunately, our predictions are just that: predictions. How many of us could have predicted a pandemic would change our way of life in little less than a year?

Bettering Yourself: Consult an Expert

Despite all the advancements in society, there are record-breaking losses in productivity and overall happiness. Why is that so? People are pushed into careers right out of high school. They continue to earn a wage, but they do not enjoy what they do. As significant and valuable as money is, it isn't the source of happiness. Otherwise, billionaires such as Bill Gates and Jeff Bezos wouldn't be getting divorced!

People fail to realize that nothing helps you attain your goals quicker than hiring a career coach. As great as it is to try to experiment with different career options, it's redundant in this day and age! Why reinvent the wheel when there are experts who have consulted hundreds or even thousands of clients? By consulting experts about your career, you save a lot of time, frustration, money, and long-term pain.

Getting sound advice from a coach isn't anything new. Every notable figure has had a consultant—from kings to political leaders to celebrities and everything in between—throughout history. Aristotle, Julius Caesar, and Queen Elizabeth—every influential person in the world—utilized the wisdom of advisors, coaches, mentors, and other experts. Why not you? Pursuing what you do without consulting others is usually a sign of insecurity and ignorance.

Before you consider hiring a personal, career, relationship, business, or financial coach or mentor, it's essential to remember that not all coaches are certified or have the expertise you may be seeking. However, there are always those who have what it takes to help you create the outcomes and plans to unlock your most significant potential, power, and purpose. There are many ways to find the right coach or mentor.

Many of us coaches are active members of the International Coaching Federation (ICF), the Institution of Leadership and Management (ILM), and other reputable organizations. You can also do an independent check of their website and social media profiles or listen to or read previous client reviews. Thousands of clients who have sought my help checked all of the above. Some even read my multi-award-winning and seven-times international best-selling books—*A Path to Wisdom, #Loneliness,* and *The Unfakeable Code*®— before booking a private consult or a business strategy session.

The meager fee for their consultancy and expert advice pays for itself in the long run. Investing in being coached and mentored is investing in you. Coaching can assist you with improving your mental and emotional well-being, dissolve conflicts in your intimate relationships, get the job you always wanted, get a promotion, grow your wealth, or even start your own business. Their expertise, coupled with their unbiased guidance, will help you achieve your goals quicker.

Some of the clients I have coached got in touch to help them grow their careers by teaching them how to hone their skills and develop their abilities. Even the most suitable candidate for any job isn't free from flaws; everyone has room for improvement. A great coach or mentor will help you figure out where you can improve, determine what you can gauge for yourself, your partner, your family, your current job, your business or organization, and show you what you can expect from your future career. Coaching helps you with self-confidence, communication, and negotiation.

Investing in being coached assists you in every aspect of your life, including looking for a new job, preparing for an important meeting, or building a personal vision of excellence. No, your coach won't find a job for you, but they will help you revamp your resume by making it more transparent, efficient, and eloquent. You'll be surprised by how much a well-written resume can improve your chances of landing a job!

Coaching can help you get the clarity to choose the right job if you want to move to a new position or a new career. Suzan, a very driven senior executive, initially sought my expertise to help her clarify her five-to-ten-year career goals. As we started her coaching journey, she wanted to identify significant work-related stressors that made her feel burnt out. One of the first things we did was clarify what she truly wanted from herself, her partner, her team, and the organization. We then identified all the possible issues that were slowing her down and taking away her energy, focus, and time. The next step was to look at what she thought she valued and what reality showed that she cherished and create a vital step-by-step plan to harmonize her inner and outer realities. We conducted many coaching and mentoring sessions and interviews and a five-day business-consultancy retreat. She was able to determine the next steps she needed to take to get precisely what she wanted.

If you are looking to go far in life, then save yourself long-term pain by investing in coaching to teach yourself meaningful life-enhancing tools and corporate social skills, such as speaking, networking, and connecting with others in meaningful ways. Coaches can do this by demonstrating a scenario where you follow suit and then helping you map out a network chart, which will help you find people in your relevant circle. Additionally, coaches can also conduct mock interviews for your dream jobs. These interviews help you practice real scenarios in a controlled setting. The coach can help you work on your flaws and highlight your strong points.

All in all, investing in being coached is an excellent way to find encouragement and support when things aren't going well. Whatever your issue may be, a coach, mentor, or therapist can help you get out of a difficult situation. My parents invested in privately tutors throughout my schooling, and these professors taught me the curriculum from at least five years ahead of the year I was in.

Seeking some of the top coaches, mentors, teachers, healers, and therapists in the world and investing in my growth helped me heal many emotional wounds. They also opened me up to new possibilities and my true purpose. Continued investment in my development created the life I now am grateful to have and share with the world. Being coachable is a skill that is wise to master.

Tony Jeton Selimi (Jeton Tony Selimi)

Growing Spiritually Enhances Your Career

The universe, with its infinite wisdom, has the answer to every question you could ever have. It's no surprise that spirituality can extend into everyday life, especially for your career. Several types of research in the fields of spirituality and vocational psychology have proposed that a person's spirituality affects their career choices in three ways:

- as an influence on their career-related likes and dislikes
- as a motivator
- as a means of support

A good coach will unify all three aspects into their coaching, mentoring, and teachings as spirituality goes hand in hand with everything else. Spirituality, in essence, is a unique experience that varies from one person to another and tends to vary between people.[1]

Spirituality and Its Effect on Emotional Support

It is imperative for people making career decisions to have a career coach helping them. Research has shown that people who feel more supported experience much higher levels of career satisfaction.[2] Having this safety net during difficult times is essential. Spirituality adds an additional tier of support. Connecting with the universe while being guided by a career coach does wonders for a person.

---

[1] Duffy, R. D. (2006). "Spirituality, Religion, and Career Development: Current Status and Future Directions," *Career Development Quarterly*, 55(1), 52–63.

[2] Colozzi, E. A., & Colozzi, L. C. (2000). "College Students' Callings and Careers: An Integrated Values-Oriented Perspective." In D. A. Luzzo (ed.), *Career Counseling of College Students: An Empirical Guide to Strategies That Work* (63–91). Washington, DC: American Psychological Association.

Spirituality and Its Effect on Interests and Values

In many fundamental career coaching and development theories, the main emphasis usually revolves around interests and values. People are asked how they develop their interests. These factors, in a nutshell, are made through years of culminating factors, such as family, personality, education, gender, and, most importantly, spirituality. People who consider themselves more spiritual lean toward jobs that help others or work toward the greater good.

Spirituality and Its Effect on Career Choices

People looking to start or switch their jobs or careers made an informed choice that is aided by their personal beliefs. Certain people believe they have a calling for a particular job. This calling is determined by circumstances and spiritual beliefs.[3]

Your spirit is a messenger of goodwill. Understanding the mechanisms of your mind and spirit can help you leverage your growth to your full potential and help you climb to greater heights. Coaching can help you get the clarity, the plan, and the willpower to empower the eight critical areas of life and hone the most vital skills. Most people fall into the illusion of saying to themselves and others, "I know this. I know how to do this. I know I can make money. I know I can have any career I want." In actuality, there is no evidence of their "knowing" existing in their reality. The only way to "know" is when your reality shows you proof of what you think you "know" already exists in your objective reality.

Life without spirituality is like a tree without leaves; it is dead. What water is to life is what spirituality is to your body, mind, and heart. Creating extraordinary results on your path to excellence

---

[3] Hill, P. C., & Pargament, K. I. (2003). "Advances in the Conceptualization and Measurement of Religion and Spirituality: Implications for Physical and Mental Health Research." *American Psychologist*, 58, 64–74.

requires an investment, a commitment, and persistence in the most significant asset: you. The knowledge you accumulate will pay dividends for the rest of your life.

When to Seek Expert Advice

No matter where you are in life, there will always be a gap between your current life and your desired life. Why? Because you are like nature, constantly evolving, building, and destroying what no longer serves you. You keep growing. No human being can escape the eight ever-evolving life cycles. If you are looking to learn a better, more efficient, and more effective way to create results, then seeking an expert's advice is wise.

You are not alone. So many successful people in the world use some form of a life coach to help them figure out what sits at the root of their repeated patterns, problems, and pains. If you are looking for answers to any life challenge, need clarity on what you want to do with your life, and don't know how to do it, then coaching is a brilliant tool.

One of the common mistakes I see people make—no matter where I am—is telling themselves that they can do everything by themselves. The truth is far from that. If your Ferrari's engine breaks down, would you attempt to fix it yourself—or would you take it to a professional car mechanic? The answer is obvious. So, why not treat yourself like a Ferrari? Invest in annual maintenance of your health, performance, productivity, and business skills. Regular, thorough checkups for what is going on in your psychology and your external reality can make a huge difference in your pursuit of excellence, fulfillment, and vision.

It always helps to have support, especially the support of an experienced professional who can aid you in getting where you want to be without wasting excess energy, money, or time.

6. Before you move on to the next chapter, here are eight things to ponder that can help you determine if investing in a coach is for you:

1. You feel stressed, lost, and uncertain about what choices to make in an ocean of infinite possibilities.

It's an undeniable scientific fact that the accumulated stresses of everyday life can damage your mental, emotional, and physical health in irreversible ways. For example, prolonged burnout, exhaustion, hurt, anxiety, and depression can lead to early aging, heart problems, and long-term disability. If you don't act, over time, the effects of the day-in, day-out grind can damage your health in irreversible ways.

No matter what professions my clients hail from, some of the everyday things I observe that cause them prolonged stress are long commutes, high-pressure workdays, looking for that special one, raising kids, not getting enough sleep or exercise, and trying to make ends meet.

If you're someone who becomes easily stressed or frustrated, trying to do things independently without any support will only add to your frustration. You will save yourself a lot of energy, and you will prevent stress and burn yourself out by getting expert advice and hiring a coach to support you along the way to achieving your objectives. A life coach will give some clarity to your path and show you techniques and exercises that will help you deal with your stress more efficiently.

Coaching is a great option if you are looking to find your way when you feel confused, lost, and uncertain of your next steps. If you have come to a point where you don't know who you are or what you want, investing in working with a great coach is the perfect starting point for your new life journey.

2. Doubt keeps stopping you from taking action, making a decision, and experiencing life to the fullest.

Working with a coach can help you find the clarity needed to build your certainty if you frequently doubt yourself. You often know what you want deep down inside, but you become confused by what the world around you projects at you. Often, many of you can't articulate what you want. My clients say, "I should do this," "I have to do this," or "I must do this." I ask hundreds of quality questions, and they come to understand how this language is simply a representation of other people's values and voids running their lives.

A great coach or mentor can hear what you cannot and masterfully help you upgrade your psychology in alignment with the life goals you want for yourself. Coaching enables you to realize what your dreams are and the best way to reach them.

3. You have a calling, a vision, and a purpose you want to realize, but you have no clear plan of action in place.

Nothing in the world that stands the test of time was built without a detailed plan. Let's take the iconic symbol of London: The Tower Bridge. The original proposal—for a bridge at a low level on the tilting principle, that is, a bridge at level with the streets, with two leaves or arms that could be raised to let the ships pass downstream and be lowered to allow vehicles to pass from one side to another through the canal—was presented in 1878 to the City of London Corporation by architect Horace Jones. In 1885, a law of Parliament was passed that empowered the City of London Corporation to build the bridge. Its construction took eight years, five main contractors, and the tireless work of 432 construction workers every day.

Like Horace Jones, many of you have a goal or vision you want to bring into this world, but you have no clue how to achieve it. Investing in hiring a coach can help you create a detailed plan, the action steps, and the momentum needed to remain committed and on course to your desired destination. Hundreds of clients who have done my five-day Vital Planning Business and Life Mastery Advanced Learning Seminar have benefited from clarifying what they want, where they are at the moment, and creating a step-by-step plan to bridge the gap between where they are now and where their heart is asking them to go. A detailed plan is a wise thing to do on your journey to realizing your dreams and extraordinary visions. Too many great ideas go unrealized due to a lack of organization and clarity, and the world misses out every time.

4. You are unhappy doing what you do. You have an unexplained desire to change your profession.

Midlife crisis is a scientifically well-researched human phenomenon. Most of us live our lives conforming to the wishes and expectations of our parents, society, and other people. At some point in your life, usually between thirty-five and fifty-five, you may experience a midlife crisis. You may realize that the life you are living is not be the life you want in your future. Thus, unexplainable feelings and desire to change start to take over you. This could be related to wanting to get out of a relationship you feel trapped in, a job that no longer fulfills you, or yearning to move to a better climate. Perhaps some of you want to start your own business or enter a new field. The expert guidance of a life coach can give you the confidence and assurance you need to take the necessary leap.

7. For those who want to learn more about some of the signs and effects of a midlife crisis, you may want to head to Amazon Prime and watch *Living My Illusion: The Truth Hurts.* This is a life-coaching documentary. If not addressed, the midlife crisis can have a nasty effect on every aspect of our reality. The inspiration to cocreate this documentary appeared when I coached my clients Joel and Timea Van der Molen. On this journey, Joel felt highly inspired to film their transformational journey with me and contribute toward

raising global awareness about the lies we tell ourselves and the masks we wear have on our bodies, minds, hearts, and souls about business leadership and parenting. Since its launch, the documentary has won more than seventeen global awards. You see, coaching can change your life, and it can help you make your dreams come true—as it has done for many of my global clients. No matter what you do, you don't feel fulfilled or meaningful.

If you want to stop struggling and feeling this way, I encourage you to use each of the Octagon of Excellence's principles to map out your blueprint to live life to the fullest. Some of you may be looking to improve your physical, emotional, or mental health. And others want to grow their businesses, create products, write books, or build one hell of a profit.

8. No matter what is going on, if you feel like you could use some advice, clarity, and guidance, you may want to hire a coach to get to where you want to be cheaper, faster, and wiser; it's best not to go it alone. You keep procrastinating, and for some reason, you don't always follow through.

How often do you tell yourself you will do something and end up not doing it? No matter how much you try, something or someone gets in the way, and before you know it, your day is filled with activities that leave you uninspired and unfulfilled. Procrastinating is your body's way of communicating that you are doing things that don't inspire, fulfill, or bring you closer to your dream life.

This is where a coach can make a huge difference in your life and keep you accountable, inspired, and on course. The fantastic thing is that tools such as Zoom, Skype, and Facebook Video enable us to be coached in the comfort of our own homes. Having an online life coach is an excellent choice if you tend to give up or downplay the importance of some of your obligations and would benefit from having someone there to remind you to finish what you started and help you stay motivated.

9.   Procrastinating is never going to get you where you want to be. Reaching your goals takes action, clarity, and discipline. It calls for getting things done on time, keeping a schedule, and having a list of inspired activities that represent what your authentic values want of you. Many clients I have consulted sought my help to help them change behavior patterns, break their habit of procrastinating, move forward, and live the lives they want. You value time, you no longer want to waste it, and you want to be financially free.

Time is your soul's most precious gift. Unfortunately, the majority of us were never told this at a young age. Many of us were not taught how to use time in the most effective ways. It is no wonder that millions, if not billions, of people waste their most precious gift: time. Does anybody have time to waste these days? Distractions take up your time—from within or outside of your outer reality.

Yes, life can be demanding and hectic, and it can throw you from one emotional river to another, from one challenging mountain to another, and from one demanding valley to another. You are running endlessly on the hamster wheel of life, wasting time going around in circles, trying to reach your goals, and using up more of your precious time. This is where working things through with a life coach or a business coach—or both—will save you time by helping you find solutions faster and keeping you on your path so that you can get to where you're going as quickly as possible.

Over the years, I have spoken at the UN and at business conferences, universities, companies from all market sectors, and at TEDx. The things that audiences want are inner peace, certainty, confidence, money, and financially independence. People are running into a common dilemma: the need for more money when they are barely making enough to survive. I have been there many times, and I know it can be challenging to break into a dream job that provides a steady income that your current circumstances may not. Each time I have helped clients unlock their wealth-building abilities, I assisted them in doing something they love.

My client story is just one of the hundreds of examples I can give you. Our paths crossed at Quantum Leap, a PR firm we both had invested in helping us grow our business. In one of their yearly events, the founder, Steve Harrison, asked me to speak about the legendary Jack Canfield, the author of one of my favorite book series, "Chicken Soup for the Soul," to share strategies for how fellow authors and entrepreneurs can authentically use social media to sell more books and build their businesses while doing what they love.

Back then, her total yearly income was $55,000. Fast-forward three years, having attended many of my five-day Vital Planning for Elevated Living custom-made business and life mastery workshops, she used this opportunity to clarify who she was, what she had to offer, heal her trauma, create a new brand that represented her more authentically, create a plan for a series of books, and increase her income by more than ten times.

You see, a great coach can squeeze out of you the knowledge that others can benefit from, direct you to resources, and share insights you need to go in a rewarding, purposeful, and profitable direction. It's a "win-win-win-win-win situation." I created this five-win formula from a series of life encounters that I used to help me and others grow, self-reflect, and focus on the value we all offer. In any life endeavor and relationship, it is wise for the focus to be on creating a win for you, a win for those you serve, and a win for humanity.

There are so many more benefits to working with a coach, mentor, or therapist than I can mention here. Life coaching, healing, mentorship, and a lot of therapy helped me heal and develop self-confidence, self-assertion, and self-love. It is why I love promoting education, coaching, and mentorship as empowering tools that every child, adult, and leader can benefit from. A coach supports you as you take risks that make your life better and helps your dreams come true. They show you that you are just as worthy of love, success, and wealth as anybody else. Choosing the right coach for your circumstances is also essential. Why? Because, in doing so, you have chosen someone who stays by your side as you gather the experience you need to believe in yourself and become more self-confident, self-efficient, and self-driven.

If any of these eight signs resonate with you, it may be time to look into hiring a mentor or a life or business coach and benefit from the services they have to offer. You will get to where you want to be more quickly when you have someone you trust to lean on for clarity, guidance and a long-term fruitful friendship. When the going gets tough, and you feel anxious, doubtful, and stressed, use principle 5: "For better, more efficient, and more effective results, seek expert advice."

9

BE IN SYNC WITH EVOLUTION

For all things are either contraries or composed of contraries,
and unity and plurality are the principles of all contrariety.
—Aristotle

Principle 6: To grow on the inside and expand on the outside, collaborate.

This quote by Aristotle is just as relevant today as it was centuries ago when it was coined. At a passing glance, it might even come off as pseudo-intellectual as a means to complicate relatively simple concepts. Yet, it takes a rather in-depth approach to comprehend and appreciate Aristotle's genius.

For starters, let's begin with what quantifies as "contrary." The contrary is the opposite; the day is contrary to the night, hot is contrary to cold, light is contrary to dark, and so forth. Our lives are nothing short of an amalgamation of contraries that have been at the forefront of our existence. All things in the universe—from the giant stars and galaxies to the smallest atoms—have their contraries. For a supermassive star, there is an equal and opposite repelling force, which is known as dark matter. Electrons will always try to reach equilibrium for every atomic structure and match the same number of protons. To have the contraries is a universal constant. Failure to do so results in disharmony and dis-ease.

There is no better example of contraries than yin and yang. Ancient Chinese philosophy dictates how this pair of opposites is actually interrelated and codependent. Chinese cosmology further expounds upon how this is a universal concept. It takes the destruction of a star (a supernova explosion) to create new stars; without this destruction, there cannot be birth.

Every part of human existence is a culmination of contraries. For every joy we celebrate, there is a sadness that follows. The fundamental contraries of life help us evolve into the best version of ourselves by accepting change.

The Octagon of Excellence considers all of this as it highlights the importance of the eight evolutionary cycles. Let's take a closer look at how we can utilize the Octagon of Excellence to help you collaborate and be in sync with your evolution. Great teams, leaders, and individuals all use collaboration to negotiate and achieve results. Those who are great at collaborating gain priceless insights from several people, faced with different aspects of the same problem. The adversary is not the person across the table. The adversary is the situation. The person across the table is a counterpart who is struggling with some aspect of the same problem that you are.

Collaborating is essential for maintaining a healthy body, being in a loving relationship, working with colleagues, and solving significant problems. Together, we are all better off.

The Octagon of Excellence and Evolution

Evolution, growth, and transformation are necessary for our lives and for the lives of every living thing. The simplest single-cell organism has to continuously evolve and grow to avoid predators, and so do the wildebeests in the African plains. Evolution is a constant process, and it resembles the principle of time.

Much like time, evolution marches forward. It is a continuous process of improvement to benefit the self and the generations that will follow. Evolution could be how rabbits evolved better hearing and fur that blends better with their surroundings. Human evolution is somewhat different. Evolution, for us, means the need to change. Change itself is the only constant in life; everything is guaranteed to change. We make and break relationships and friendships. We find new jobs, leave old positions, and become entrepreneurs who solve global problems. Society has become more accepting, open, and tolerant toward ethnic minorities and indigenous and LGBTQ+ communities. Just a few decades ago, we were not. We have become concerned about important matters like human rights and global warming.

The best way to know if you're on the right track of growth and evolution is by asking yourself, "Have I learned something new today?" Maybe you practiced an existing skill (perhaps you practiced the guitar today) or picked up a new skill altogether (you began to learn how to play the guitar). As long as you can proudly say, "Yes, today I learned _____" every day, you are evolving toward becoming the best version of yourself.

The next step is what you do with what you have learned. This is not limited to a skill set. If you learned something in a book, an exciting fact online, or about how pollution affects the environment, you have taken the first step toward reaching your maximum potential. Maybe you learned how bad plastic straws are for marine life. If you now choose to avoid using plastic straws altogether (using either a metal or bamboo variant), you have successfully implemented the knowledge you learned and evolved into an improved version of yourself. This process is continuous. As long as there is life in your body, you can improve yourself for your benefit and for the benefit of everyone associated with you.

This is where the collaborative spirit comes into play. Humans are social animals. The technological marvels we see today in our daily lives are the culmination of thousands upon thousands of years of human evolution and growth. Because of this very collaborative effort, I can write this book on my computer. If I were to explain what a computer was to someone from 1950, they would think I was insane. Yet, here we are! Thanks to the collaborative effort of humanity, we have learned to grow both inside and outside as the best versions of ourselves.

Interpersonal growth is at the forefront of human evolution. It is through unity and collaborative effort that the best eras of humanity have surfaced. The Renaissance was a time where new ideas occurred in all manners of society: physics, chemistry, biology, art, and philosophy. These masters flourished in this era and paved the way for most (if not all) of our modern-day amenities. The world would be a much different place without the works of da Vinci, Galileo, Descartes, Michelangelo, and dozens of others.

Through the collaboration of preceding generations, we have achieved success as a species. Now, let's see how we can utilize the Octagon of Excellence for this:

Tony Jeton Selimi (Jeton Tony Selimi)

Transition

Transition into the best version of yourself by continuously evolving your mindset for the collective benefit of every living being on our planet.

Regeneration

Regenerate your beliefs—and let nothing remain stagnant. Continuous improvement is dependent on regeneration because it allows you to change and improve yourself.

Focus

It is impossible to change yourself if you don't apply yourself. There is no better way to do so than to focus on becoming the best version of yourself. Focus on your growth, both intrinsic and extrinsic.

Rebirth

To gain something, we must lose something. The cycle of life dictates death and rebirth. This transcends the physical plain and establishes itself in the metaphysical. To grow intrinsically and extrinsically, be willing to "rebirth" through every transient life predicament into your most authentic self.

Balance

Yin and yang. Remember the Aristotelian principle of contraries? There is a bad for every good, just like Newton's law of every action having an equal and opposite reaction. Life's balance includes good and evil, which one you give power to defines who you become.

Service

Service includes the help and guidance you offer to everyone associated with you.

Unity

Unity matters for society and humanity in general. We are where we are today because of the collective efforts of society, and unity will help us climb to even greater heights.

Infinity

It is vital to know that the infinite expanse of the universe promotes growth and evolution as it undergoes the same process. Promoting expansion and change is the natural flow of the universe.

Law of the One

One of the universal principles perceived by inquisitive and more deeply thinking human beings in the universe—and one of the most fundamental, omnipresent laws of nature—is the law of the one and the many.

The premise of this principle has been a fundamental part of human evolution for millennia. It is interrelated with nearly every discipline of every field. In essence, it consists of the primary, foundational laws of human thought, decision, perception, and action. This law is worth the contemplation and thought it garners.

The law itself states, "From the one come the many, and from the many come the one." The two contraries work together in harmony. In this instance, the interconnection of the many and the one is highlighted. Any attempts to remove either will cause havoc.

The law of unity and multiplicity forms the base understanding of astronomy. It dictates how the universe started with the big bang and how it is always expanding. Einstein's theoretical ideas of gamma photons (one) having the ability to create more particles (many) have been proven true.

In biology and chemistry, many reactions can occur to make one product (for example, the production of salt), and one product can also result in many reactions (such as an explosion). These concepts are intertwined with the human psyche. A person could be attracted to one, such as a romantic partner, while simultaneously being repelled by "many," such as their romantic partner's disapproving friends!

Let's see how this has real-world implications. If you own a business (one) and mistreat your customers (many), this will result in you going out of business. If you treat them well, you will gain business. Similarly, if you undergo economic hardships (as many of us have due to COVID), your customers (many) can help lift your business (one) out of turmoil and put you on the right track.

Among your friends, if you (one) told them (many) that you were feeling sad, they would do their best to cheer you up. Yet, if all you ever did was use your friends for your benefit, you would soon find yourself without any.

The world around us—and even our intrinsic thought process— is a mirror reflection of the law of the one and the many. Ponder this as much as you can—and make sure you start to see this correlation in every single aspect of your life. The more you correlate it with real-life scenarios, the easier it will become to have more realistic expectations from people, providing you a competitive edge among your peers.

Mortimer Adler said, "Those who do not deny either the unity of being or its multiplicity tend to make the primary fact about reality either its oneness or its manyness."

Any form of fear, judgment, or criticism can easily isolate you from the very same people with whom you can grow. Thus, remind yourself of principle 6: "To grow on the inside and expand on the outside, collaborate."

10

WHAT GOES AROUND COMES AROUND

Principle 7: To unleash the power of gratitude, graciously give and accept compliments.

Regardless of your stance on religion or spirituality, you have probably heard of karma. Karma, or the law of karma, makes up the universal laws that govern our experiences of the world. The law of the universe is absolute—without any errors and without the need for any amendments. When we adhere to those rules, we allow ourselves to channel the universe's perfection into our very being. To accomplish that to the best of our abilities, let us first understand what karma is.

Karma is an ancient law that has existed in various human cultures for thousands of years. In a nutshell, the law of karma discusses how every single aspect of our lives is energy. This includes—but is not limited to—our thoughts, actions, emotions, expressions, and mannerisms. Everything we do creates karma, good or bad—a positive or negative consequence.

In essence, karma allows individuals to be more mindful of their day-to-day actions, right down to their very mindsets and thinking patterns. There are twelve fundamental laws of karma:

The Law of Cause and Effect

This is the fundamental law of karma, which summarizes the entirety of it. This is also what people most commonly refer to when they talk about karma. According to the teachings of this law, whatever you do, you get in return. If you are good to someone, you get "good" in return (and vice versa).

The Law of Creation

This law signifies the importance of existence. If we ponder over our lives, being born and existing in itself is no less than a miracle. Our lives simply did not happen by chance, and we need to take action to attain something rather than waiting for it to magically fall from the sky.

The Law of Humility

This law focuses on being humble about your situation in life. It is about knowing and acknowledging that whatever you are experiencing today is due to a culmination of your previous actions, thoughts, and intentions. Be humble about your situations.

The Law of Growth

Like every seed grows into its plant, it's wise for you to focus on yourself before focusing on others. Real growth begins from the one thing you have absolute control over: yourself.

The Law of Responsibility

Simply put, most of your predicaments are due to the result of your actions. Learn to take responsibility for dealing with whatever life throws at you.

The Law of Connection

Everything in your life is interconnected with your past, present, and future. The person you are today is due to the culmination of events that molded you into who you are (and who you will be).

The Law of Focus

This law emphasizes the importance of focusing on one thing at a time. Whatever you focus on, you will attract—so it is best to keep your attention turned toward the positive.

The Law of Giving and Hospitality

Giving in this sense equates to all the positive aspects of your life and how you can spread them to those who lack it. This can mean anything from food and shelter to those who lack it to something as simple as a smile for someone who is sad.

The Law of Here and Now

Learn from the past and plan for the future, but focus on the present. Remember, the life you are living at this very moment is the life you worked all those years for.

The Law of Change

History tends to repeat itself until you learn from it and actively change yourself to better suit your surroundings and environment. Change is a fundamental part of life.

The Law of Patience and Reward

"Good things come to those who wait" is a famous saying for apparent reasons. Sometimes, you have to let the pieces fall into place and wait for karma to take its route.

The Law of Significance and Inspiration

Just as a single drop of ink can change the color of water, each person is significant and can shape and influence their surroundings.

Now that we have established some information about the twelve laws of karma, let's discuss the first (and most important) law of karma: the law of cause and effect.

The Law of Cause and Effect

If you think back to your high school physics class, you might remember Newton's third law: "For every action, there is an equal and opposite reaction." Newton was referring to this in the scientific aspect, but thousands of years before he discovered this, the teachings of karmic law discussed its importance for everything.

In a nutshell, every effect in your life has a cause, and every cause creates an effect. By aligning your thoughts and monitoring your actions, you can make the cause (the action/reason that brings about the results) coincide with your effect (the result of an action or cause). In the 1980s, when I was studying physics, math, biology, chemistry, and other life sciences, I first came across these laws. Back then, no one knew or spoke about how Newton's laws and other universal laws relate to our daily life. Even today, children and students are taught many beautiful things, yet most educational institutions fail to teach them in a relatable way.

Imagine how much more we could collectively achieve, how much healthier we would be, and how much more aware we would be if we knew how to apply these laws to help us change our internal dialogue and transform our attitudes, behaviors, thoughts, and being? Many more of us would start to harness the power, purpose, and profits that this law can unleash in our lives and other people's lives.

To fully enjoy what the universe has to offer, we require to overcome our self-imposed limits, which can be done by applying the law of cause and effect to our daily lives.

By being mindful of our deeds, thoughts, and actions, we become more conscious of our surroundings and stop divulging in reckless behavior. It's easier to understand this law by taking some practical examples of karma at work:

- A person helps someone with their startup, and when it becomes successful, as a token of thanks, they make them a stockholder.
- The teacher goes out of the way to help their students. In turn, the students recommend the teacher, and they get a promotion.
- An employee makes a mistake but admits to it and fixes it instead of hiding it. They are then offered a promotion for their honesty.

The Gratitude Effect

Now that we've established how vital "good karma" is, let's discuss what makes it worthwhile: gratitude. Gratitude is about being appreciative. This can be about literally anything in your life. You can be grateful for your past, present, and future. The effects of gratitude are so profound that they can physically benefit you.

Two psychologists, Dr. Michael E. McCullough (University of Miami) and Dr. Robert A. Emmons (University of California, Davis), conducted research on gratitude. They asked participants to write a few sentences about specific topics. One group wrote things related to gratefulness, another wrote about what irritated them, and a third group wrote neutral things. After ten weeks, the group that wrote more about gratitude felt better about themselves and was overall more optimistic. Surprisingly, they were the ones who tended to exercise more and had fewer visits to the doctor.

Although this might seem far-fetched, there is actual science to back up how practicing gratitude can benefit your health. By being grateful, we reduce the leading cause of most health problems: stress.[4] Once a person can counter stress, they can effectively improve their mental health.

Gratitude is food for the soul. The more you practice it, the better you will feel about yourself and your surroundings and situations. Make a habit of thanking others for their efforts, thank your friends and family for supporting you, and most importantly, thank yourself for working on the biggest asset of your life: you.

Perhaps the most excellent way to practice and spread gratitude is by complimenting others and yourself. I like to categorize compliments into two types: extrinsic and intrinsic. Extrinsic compliments focus on outward aspects, such as someone complimenting your clothes,

---

[4] Ryff, C. D., Singer, B. H., & Dienberg Love, G. (2004). *Positive Health: Connecting Well-Being with Biology.* Philosophical Transactions of the Royal Society of London. Series B: Biological Sciences, 359 (1449). https://doi.org/10.1098/rstb.2004.1521.

hair, or car. On the other hand, intrinsic compliments primarily focus on your achievements and accomplishments, being commended for your work ethic, determination, attention to detail with your work, and everything related to who you are as a person.

When you receive either type of compliment, it might get a little embarrassing, especially if you are not used to hearing it. At the same time, it offers an opportunity to explore and appreciate a part of you that you may not have paid attention to. Similarly, complimenting others can provide them with the same feeling of self-satisfaction while maintaining good karma for both of you.

Karma and the Octagon of Excellence

Transition

Accepting compliments and becoming more gracious helps you transition into the best version of yourself as you allow positivity to flow in and expunge negativity from your body and soul.

Regeneration

There is no better way to cheer up and feel good about yourself than to be happy, and the quickest way to be happy is to be appreciated for your efforts. Simple compliments and mindfulness can help mend your mindset and help you regenerate from negativity and harm.

Focus

A positive outlook on life helps you focus on everything important to you—your work or your life—and it even helps you look forward to your future.

Rebirth

Remember cause and effect. By establishing a positive outlook, we effectively are reborn into a more upbeat version of ourselves.

Balance

Life is a balance of good and evil. The only acceptable way to "tip the scale" is toward the good side. Don't feel shy or hesitant to do good because whatever good you do to maintain balance will be given to you tenfold.

Service

Embracing positivity is doing service to yourself and those around you. You create a warm, welcoming aura around you that makes it possible for everyone who associates with you to indulge in the benefits of being positive, including health benefits.

Unity

Positivity increases unity with your surroundings, the universe, and whatever you believe to be your Creator. You will feel more authentic, grounded, stable, focused, and ready for everything. You will become a beacon that will emanate this energy for those in need.

Infinity

The best thing about giving and receiving compliments is that there is no end to it. Positivity is similar to life. It is fleeting. Unlike negativity, which oozes like toxic mold, positivity is like a butterfly on a flower. It rests on the petals, replenishes itself with the nectar, and is on its way, making room for other butterflies to take advantage of the infinite supply of positivity.

If you find yourself not celebrating other people's personal, relationship, professional, business, financial, or social achievements, remind yourself to use principle 7: "To unleash the power of gratitude, graciously give and accept compliments."

11

LEVERAGE THE POWER OF ACKNOWLEDGING YOUR ACHIEVEMENTS

Principle 8: Continuously celebrating small wins can change your physiology, strengthen your psychology, and maximize your potential.

Sometimes, it gets challenging for us to keep ourselves motivated on the thorny path of success. Our journey becomes hugely exhausting and frustrating, and we continue facing the same obstacles. Every day seems like a battle with little to no hope, excessive stress, and anxiety. Our mind keeps rehashing those negative thoughts, and we feel like giving up.

This common scenario reminds me of the saying of a fictional German hero. Baron Munchausen says, "Trying to sustain your drive through a task, a project, or even a career can sometimes feel like pulling yourself out of a swamp by your hair." Most of us naturally possess an almost infinite capacity of aversion toward tenacity and persistence, and no amount of caffeine or counselors can fix that.

What is the solution to this pessimistic approach? Well, in my opinion, life is a continuous battle of unavoidable challenges and hardships. Every day, we wake up with a new problem in our minds, no matter how much we try to avoid it. I believe that inspiration and encouragement are the only two easy solutions to implement in these harsh circumstances. It might sound a bit cliché, but that is all you need to make through all the dark times. However, there's a little technique that's attached to boosting these superpowers. Want to know more about it? Let's take a look.

Researchers have found that you need to remind yourself of your small wins to feel more uplifted and inspired. It helps you boost your self-esteem and strengthens your self-belief. Your small wins make you realize how you have been progressing like a champ throughout the whole process and haven't given up. If you are struggling to achieve a long-term goal of overcoming a considerable barrier, then you may have forgotten the importance of celebrating your little wins. If you do not cheer for your everyday achievements, that's where everything goes wrong!

We all need to go easy on the idea of being a perfectionist and relax a bit. No matter how difficult the situation, you need to look at your journey and appreciate yourself for all your accomplishments. Never underestimate the power of celebrating your small wins. There is so much gratitude and bliss hidden in acknowledging your tiny everyday advancements. It keeps reminding you why you are worth it and how far you have come. For example, if you aim to lose thirty pounds, you need to set a reward plan for yourself. You can opt for excellent shopping, dining out with your friends, or enjoying a nice spa day.

The little rewards and treats can prove to be the most motivational ones. For example, you can save two or three bucks in a jar for every five pounds you lose, and at the end of your journey, you can enjoy some crazy stuff with that money. How cool is that! Your little wins keep reminding you about how far you have come and that you are wildly capable of achieving whatever you want in life. The primary key is to encourage yourself to feel even more enthusiastic and optimistic about chasing your goals. You need to practice positive affirmations each day and train your mind to think, *I can do this—and I will do it!*

As Kai Ashley puts in, "Start acknowledging all the good you are doing. Don't discount the little things. I mean, how many times do you scold yourself for doing something small that wasn't perfect? How often do you think the good things, such as being on time or signing a new client, are simply how it's meant to be? They need celebrating. You need more wins in your life. This will motivate you, encourage you, and help you see how brilliant you truly are."

We all need to be enthusiastic about our dreams and desires. They give us the power to think more positively while making important decisions. The people who possess an optimistic mindset celebrate even their little joys with as much happiness as they celebrate the bigger ones. Following your heart's callings in life allows you to put effort into your work. Therefore, even your small wins matter a lot to you. Like they say, "Happiness does not lie in the big things, but the little ones."

We often forget the challenges we have overcome, the feeling they brought us, and our learnings due to overcoming them. Most of us are victims of this mindset, and it is harmful to personal growth in the long run. If you genuinely want to be successful at something, you need to remain hopeful about the outcome of your efforts. According to scientific research, celebrating your wins feels great physically and reinforces the behavior you want to show up in a new challenge or opportunity.

Your little celebrations have the power to increase the serotonin levels in your body, which releases the happy hormones that make you feel better. This celebration mindset can be labeled as mental, emotional, and biological. The human body is designed to help you create the happiness, the contentment, and the joy you seek. No matter what you are going through, celebrating your small victories can quickly put your hormones at work—and you will feel immense pleasure within yourself with every achievement.

When you accomplish something and don't take the time to celebrate it, you rob yourself of a powerful feeling that reinforces your abilities, self-belief, confidence, and success. So much of what we do in our personal or business lives is driven (or limited) by psychology. Therefore, if you fail to celebrate your many accomplishments, you train your brain that what you are doing isn't that exciting or essential. If every day feels mundane—even when you're crushing it—you will stop giving 110 percent of yourself, which leads to lackluster results. In other words, the lack of celebration will lead to a feeling of emptiness that will result in less focus and decreased performance.

I love how children get so excited about small things. Their celebration mindset keeps them joyful and enthusiastic about life. However, children usually lose their happiness as they grow up. Do you know why? The answer is obvious. They fall for the scam of only celebrating grand victories, and it steals their joy of life. It's pretty strange how those same kids celebrate the little fun in their childhood, but it becomes difficult to get excited about things that do not qualify as big and significant once they grow up. Their idea about wins completely transforms.

We can fail to get excited about little things because we care about others' thoughts and say about us. Ask yourself, "Why do I limit my growth and happiness to impress others who simply don't care and are just as flawed as I am?" There's nothing wrong with getting excited about little things. Let your inner child come out.

Why It's Wise to Celebrate Your Accomplishments

Because the Small Triumphs Matter Too

When we think of celebrations, we think of big life moments. However, we fail to celebrate the small triumphs in our lives. We all have different life goals. For example, being consistent and determined about our weight loss journey, financial freedom journey, or learning a new dance move takes a lot of effort. A pound lost, a dollar saved, or a new personal record could be highly impactful for your overall goal. You need to celebrate any amount of progress because it indicates that you are closer to your dreams. A wise thing to do is to implement this habit in your everyday life as well. Your accomplishments, big or small, are impactful to your success and deserve to be acknowledged.

Celebrating every win can encourage you to perform even better in the future. Acknowledging your success will fuel the motivation within you to keep pushing forward. It can evoke a more positive attitude about your tasks and help you become more aligned with your goals. Writing in a success journal can help you look back and remind yourself that you have been moving toward your goals with every step you take.

Sharing your celebrations can inspire others to do the same thing. They want to indulge in the same motivation and happiness you are experiencing. By promoting this habit, you encourage others to celebrate their accomplishments. Overall, we spread positivity and motivation in our communities. It strengthens your network. Sharing your win story can stimulate new ideas and opportunities in your circle. Someone may be in the same situation as you were, leading to them accomplishing their goals. Another person in your network may have a practical idea, giving you a new way to implement it in your practice.

Confidence Booster

Celebrating small wins can drastically boost your confidence levels. When you acknowledge what you are good at, you become more confident about yourself. You will more likely continue doing what you are good at. You can praise the great things that make you who you are. Please acknowledge that you deserve it for every goal you achieve due to your skills, hard work, and dedication. As Dalai Lama states, "With the realization of one's potential and self-confidence in one's ability, one can build a better world. Recognize your strengths and use them to your advantage." I can't agree more with his statement.

Celebrating your accomplishments means celebrating yourself. Needless to say, celebrations tend to increase happiness levels. It's easy to honor those around you and fail to acknowledge your wins. Sometimes, we do not give ourselves the same love and respect that we provide to others. This way of behaving contributes to giving your power away. A wise thing to do is value your efforts and appreciate your progress so that you can feel better about your journey. It will ease the process for you. Whether it's dinner with friends, buying something you've been eyeing, or taking a day to pamper yourself, take that time to enjoy how far you've come. We can get into the pattern of constantly going, and it can get overwhelming when we only focus on the bigger picture. Celebrate how far you've come and all that you've achieved.

Self-belief and confidence are closely related. You cannot celebrate your victories unless you start valuing your present— just like your past. You need to have faith in yourself and trust the process like a champ. Keep reminding yourself that there are absolutely no barriers in this world that can stop you from getting to your dream destination. Deep down, you know that you possess the extraordinary skills, willpower, and strength to make the present more beautiful than your past. Just be strong and keep moving forward. Never give up on yourself. You have to fight for your goals.

Make sure you keep taking regular slots from your busy schedule to monitor and analyze your performance. You need to enjoy all those flashback moments when you achieve all those things that you once considered undoable or tough. This will make you realize how strong you have become. You will feel an instant boost of self-belief and keep moving forward with the same spirit.

Celebrations are all about lifting your confidence levels so that you can accept yourself with all your flaws. There's no point in changing yourself for anyone else. Just be yourself. Keep winning and be the happiest person in your circle. Because why not? What's stopping you from celebrating your wins? Trust me. It can change your whole life. The key is to have faith that these times are going to bring a big blessing for you.

Kelly Rowland says, "We all have different things that we go through in our everyday life, and it's really important to know just at the end of the day, it doesn't matter what you face, you know that you're going to win at the end of the day. You got to believe in yourself. You got to believe in God, know that He's going to get you through it."

Attracting More Wins

According to researchers, celebrating your small wins can drastically increase optimism in your life, leading to even more accomplishments. When you see yourself winning already, you become even more motivated to achieve your main goal. Positive thinkers tend to keep going even in challenging circumstances because they do not fear adversity. Instead, they face it with full strength and confidence. You become bold and fearless about your choices, which helps you make better life decisions. You can keep better track of your progress this way.

Celebrating your accomplishments means celebrating yourself. It encourages you to keep fighting for your goals. Most of the time, we focus so much on other people's achievements that we forget to notice how far we have come. We find it easy to honor those around us because their wins are more visible.

Becoming Happier

According to Jungian psychologist Dr. James Hollis, our quest for happiness is not the focus of our lives. Instead, it would be best for us to design a life that revolves around its meaning. Why is the agenda of happiness mentioned in nearly every motivational article and blog? The answer is simple. It is something that we all want in our lives—no matter what. Hollis says, "Joy and happiness are not goals in themselves, but they are the by-product of those moments when we are doing what is right for us."

When you are constantly achieving your small goals and making some smashing progress, your inner self keeps hinting that things are going the right way. That's how your serotonin levels get at work, and you feel that instant happiness within yourself. Your joy is a by-product of your timely achievements. Therefore, you need to celebrate the small wins and promote feelings of happiness in your life. Your progress cannot be ignored; you need to appreciate yourself for being on the right track!

Celebrating your little wins is a proven way to add more happiness to your life. There is so much charm in keeping an eye on your progress and appreciating yourself—even if nobody else is doing it for you. For example, how about treating yourself to nice ice cream or a movie night occasionally? It can play a significant role in uplifting your mood instantly and motivating you to perform even better. Just do more of what makes you happy—as long as it's healthy.

Promoting Self-Love

This is the most crucial point in this chapter—and I don't know where to start. Over the years, I have learned that self-love is the best medicine for all physical, mental, emotional, and social problems. This little trick of falling in love with yourself can go a long way toward keeping you at peace. Honestly, there is no good reason for you not to love yourself. No matter what corner of the world you live in, I am sure you are a hard worker and follow some "dream paths" to achieve your goals. Even if nobody believes in you, you have been making fantastic progress—and you deserve all the love!

Humans have a tendency to learn from our mistakes and make even more progress as time goes by. You have been learning all your way, and you deserve to be rewarded for this. Don't forget to pour tons of self-love into your life. Why is it so unusual to fall for other people and not yourself? What is so wrong with it? Life is too short to be miserable and hard on yourself. You need to go easy on the idea of being a perfectionist and forgive yourself for making mistakes.

My dad used to say, "People make mistakes because they are learning. No mistakes indicate that you are not trying." And he was right. If you have been making many mistakes lately or have made tons of errors in the past, know that you are a champ because you are trying! Unlike millions of other people, you dared to take a stand for yourself and start your transformation journey—that, in itself, is an achievement. So, stop fretting about the outcomes and go easy on the idea of being right all the time. It is okay to be wrong sometimes; we are all equally flawed. Nobody is perfect.

Whether it's dinner with friends, buying something you've been eyeing, or taking a day to pamper yourself, take the time to enjoy how far you've come. By adopting this small practice, you can get into a pattern of constantly going forward. It can get overwhelming if you keep focusing on the bigger picture. You need to stop doing that and celebrate how far you've come and all that you've achieved with your immense hard work and continuous efforts. It is all going to pay off in the end, and you will be so proud of yourself for not giving up—even when times were not in your favor.

Pouring self-love into your life is a powerful way to demonstrate that you notice how amazing you are. It promotes feelings of gratefulness within you and makes you learn how to rely on your positive feedback rather than looking to the outside world to appreciate you. It might sound a little funny, but I think that nobody in the world would promote the theory that "people pleasing is the gateway to the kingdom of joy." Stop waiting for other people to tell you how incredibly precious, intelligent, and valuable you are—and start acknowledging all your little successes as you walk on your dream path. Kick out all the toxic and damaging people from your life and create your empire. I am sure you can do it!

When you practice self-love, your self-esteem improves drastically because you get to realize your true worth. Try to maintain a daily log of your little victories. At the end of the week, you can read everything you celebrated; it will help you so much in keeping track of whatever good you have been doing that week. It will encourage you to keep going and not give up on your goal. To enjoy even a more significant win, read your celebration journal again at the end of the year. You will be more than amazed.

A charming teacher in high school used to ask us to pat our backs whenever we performed well on tests or other activities, and we used to feel so good about it! She used to say, "Achieving high marks on your tests is your progress reminder that you are committed to graduating from high school and that you are doing so well." Although it was such a small act, it still gives me goose bumps to remember all of us patting our own backs and laughing with each other. It has been many years, but that pat has never left me. I try to keep reminding myself of it every day.

What's more impressive was that she used to do our regular counseling and emphasized the importance of practicing self-love. She explained that there would hardly be any people telling us how far we have come or what kind of progress we have been making.

"It's you—and always you—who needs to take the responsibility of praising yourself, even in the darkest days."

Our attitudes toward our problems determine how far we can go. Try to remain as positive as possible and stay calm while walking on your dream path. I would love it if you would follow that pat routine; you will fall in love with yourself and your journey.

Finally, I want to remind you that it is okay to be different. It's okay to take breaks, but make giving up is not an option. Just eliminate the shit from your life—and keep going. You've got this!

A person who feels appreciated, cared for, and loved will always do more than what is expected. May principle 8 support you on your journey to overcome obstacles and reach excellence in whatever your heart calls you to be: "Continuously celebrating small wins can change your physiology, strengthen your psychology, and maximize your potential."

12

YOU ARE DESTINED FOR BRILLIANCE—HONOR IT

It's up to you to give yourself permission to do something extraordinary for yourself, others, the world, and the universe. You would not be given an unlimited power without the ability to use it to fulfill your innermost aspirations, desires, and callings.

Over the years, I realized that one of the biggest tragedies in life is not failing at something; it is giving up on your dreams, vision, and mission in life due to eight primary forms of fear or guilt that come from subordinations to perceived authorities in each of the eight areas of life: spiritual, mental, physical, emotional/love, vocational/business, financial, familial, and social.

These eight fears manifest in different forms in your life and make other people's approvals, judgments, and rejections so powerful. That stops you from overcoming ever-evolving life setbacks and growing into your true potential.

To pull this inner yearning out of your authentic being, do not let any of the eight primary forms of fear or guilt cloud your clarity of revelation or inhibit your determination of what your path to excellence truly entails. Instead, you can use what you fear the most to discover or awaken the true greatness residing in the divinity of your nature. Begin to clarify these fears, look at how they serve you, and take steps to overcome them. Write an inspiring life mission that is aligned to your authentic values and dedicate your life to rewriting, continually refining, and living your divinity-driven mission for the remainder of your life.

The next time you feel like you cannot achieve a particular goal or outcome, remind yourself that those barriers exist only in your mind—and you have the power to break through them. If you have established notions and misconceptions of not growing, transforming, and winning at life, this is the moment to change them. Most of the time, people become so anxious about the outcome that they don't even dare to step into the journey. And that's where things go wrong! Your success lies at the end of your comfort, which I love to call the "familiar zone."

Unwillingly, many of you may have become victims of your fake persona's attitudes, beliefs, and doubts that you cannot achieve more than a specific limit. You have been programmed to hold on to transient identities and bound yourself by restricting your vision, which undermines your efforts and the potential to achieve excellence. You conceal the infinity of your divinity from the fear of showing to the world your authentic self. So who has set these limits in your mind? Who has told you that these are your boundaries and that you cannot achieve more than this? Whose voice are you listening to in your head?

None of us come to this world with a manual of clear instructions for what we can do and can't do—and neither did our parents or the people who achieved extraordinary things in life and ended up improving humanity forever. If you are always looking at the bigger picture, at ways of assisting others in fulfilling their aspirations, and have an attitude of gratitude, success will always knock on your door. You are free to explore your choices and learn from your experiences. You can steer your path in any direction; it may as well be the one that leads toward your highest potential.

Take a moment to self-reflect, analyze your current situation, and ask yourself if you are genuinely content inside. Are you accomplishing all that you have dreamed of? What is your ultimate goal? If you had any superpower, what would that be? What things do your heart and soul call you to do? Do you seek better physical health, a loving relationship, or a home to settle down in? Are you looking to build a career that fulfills you, create a thriving business, become financially independent, or dedicate your life's work to a cause that inspires you? Is your dream to be a popular singer like Ed Sheeran, Justin Bieber, Rita Ora, Dua Lipa, or Demi Lovato?

Regardless of your answer, the wise thing is to self-reflect and observe with objectivity how much you can benefit from successfully breaking through the mental barriers that limit your horizons. When I was in the midst of the civil war, I could not see a way out. However, what I could see in my mind's eye was the vision that I would travel the world and teach and help others someday. The same image was with me when I found myself homeless and hopeless on the streets of London, finding my first job, receiving my first paycheck, taking my university entry exams, and having my first promotion.

I vividly remember every life setback I thought I would never be able to overcome. The more I became a master of breaking my mental barriers and limits, the more I wanted to help others do the same. I realized that achieving something that we think is impossible is a very liberating and empowering feeling. It also enables you to grow your confidence, certainty, and capabilities. I have used what I have learned to help others do the same for the past thirty years. If you still doubt yourself at this point on our journey together, let me put your mind at peace. A plethora of scientific research demonstrates how you become a more refined and confident individual who is ready to take over the world each time you conquer something you thought was impossible.

By reading, absorbing, and applying what I have shared in this book, you've realized that you don't need to spend your life stuck in an illusionary inner prison; there's no point in assuming that you aren't enough. Remind yourself frequently that you a by-product of a divine intelligence and have a unique purpose to carry out in this world. Your excellence cannot be achieved by anyone else but you. You are divinely creative, intelligent, and precious!

Regardless of your aspirations and goals—and wherever you might need to start—just embark on your transformational journey today. Do not hesitate to change; that's the only way you will ever get to live an adventurous, content, and love-infused life. A thousand-mile journey begins with an action, a choice, a decision, and a first step. You'll never know how fiercely capable and powerful you are unless you encounter a difficult situation. When you do, make it your mission to learn, grow, and transform yourself from every situation that you find yourself in. It is in your darkest times that you have the opportunity to unleash your natural capabilities, potential, and strength.

Your journey from pain to purpose, from fear to freedom, from not having to having, and from living to make ends meet to achieving financial independence will benefit you, your loved ones, and thousands of others in your surroundings. It can encourage them to keep going in their worst times. I speak to you as someone who overcame bullying, sexual abuse, severe health challenges, the atrocities of a civil war, poverty, homelessness, loneliness, an identity crisis, lack of education, imposter syndrome, and redundancy. I am called to share what I have learned through books, talks, trainings, films, and documentaries to help billions of people awaken the authentic power of their divinity.

I believe that we all have an infinite ability to change, succeed, and transform. No matter how difficult the situation gets, we have an innate desire to turn things around by giving our all. We are all born with unique gifts. We can live extraordinary lives and brighten the world with our superpowers. That makes all of us brilliant, unfakeable, and beautiful in our own ways. We have been born with exceptional abilities that can help us navigate the never-ending cycles of challenge and support, build and destroy, and contract and expand when we awaken them.

Since you have been destined for excellence since birth and have been growing into your potential, some essential traits can help you reach your goals faster. If you are committed, persistent, and resilient while pursuing your innermost desires, you are bound to thrive.

As a conscious species, we can imagine, create visions, innovate, and reach a level of transformation not seen in the animal world. Therefore, it is wise to value yourself and have faith in your abilities to reach your highest goals. Each of the eight principles of the Octagon of Excellence will assist you as you go through life's transitional cycles and break through your doubts and fears. If you ever feel like you are not doing well in life or aren't achieving your expectations, consider taking another route—but remain committed to the callings of your authentic and unfakeable self. Learn to treasure your dreams and desires. You have every right to live a happy, healthy, prosperous, and meaningful life.

Judging by the photos and videos I post on social media from various beautiful locations worldwide, many people may say I was born lucky. They think that is why I keep growing and succeeding in every critical area of life—no matter the challenge—but the truth is far from that. It is the result of overcoming, conquering, and transforming challenge after challenge, doubt after doubt, and fear after fear to create an evolving wonderful life, which I feel blessed and grateful to have.

The journey to excellence and growing into your greatest potential is so much more rewarding when you have a loving partner, friend, family member, teacher, mentor, or business partner who believes in the beauty of your dreams. Put in the energy, time, and resources needed to create your wildest dreams.

On that note, I want to say a big thank you to all of the people who have been on this journey with me, especially you, the reader, and my NHS (National Health Service UK) hero, partner, and best friend, Dr. Sc. Todorche Stamenov. Your devotion, inspiration, and unconditional love throughout all the challenges life puts before us are like a warm ray of sunshine on a cold winter day.

If you feel alone in life, find the time to invest your energy in creating meaningful connections, friendships, and partnerships. Just imagine how much we could collectively achieve as a society if we genuinely encouraged each other to live a life full of fulfilled dreams, hopes, and heart callings that change other people's lives. If, like me, you travel the world speaking, training, coaching, consulting businesses, and teaching people, you'll come to realize how millions of people, if not billions, have given up on their dreams.

For whatever reason, many people fail to bring their innermost callings, desires, and visions into the physical world. They never got a chance to unleash their full strength and transform their lives with authentic choices. I felt so called to write this book so we could continue to climb to greater heights, grow into our full potential, and use what we master to leave a better world for the generations to come.

The problem many people have is giving in to distractions, falling for baseless assumptions, fears, and being driven by the fake persona's temporary pleasures and not by the callings of your authentic nature, which is divine. It took my client a lot of courage to create the finances she needed to attend the quarterly Vital Planning Business and Life Mastery Retreats. Her commitment led her to clarify who she was, what she wanted, and what sustainable products and services she needed to create to grow her business and become financially independent. In obliging to her heart's voice, she ended up making a clear brand, a step-by-step plan to a series of relationship books, and embody the universal and scientific principles I have been teaching thousands of people to solidify the belief in the beauty and the importance of her dreams.

On this life mastery transformation journey, she realized that every time I challenged her to climb to greater heights, her default response was focusing on losing something and being blinded to its gain. As we unraveled and defused what was hidden behind stressful reactions, she started to acknowledge how what frustrated her was also benefiting her. We worked on defusing emotional charges and transforming her language, thought patterns, and perceptions so that when she finds herself in challenging situations, she can objectively analyze each situation before jumping to conclusions that caused her long-term pain in the past.

We all have the power to overcome any obstacles that come our way. Your body, mind, heart, and soul will never be burdened by more than they can bear. The solution to each problem can be found somewhere within you and by having the courage to seek the help of people who specialize in what we want to overcome. While self-work is essential, do not be fooled by the illusion that you can do it all by yourself. Different professions, skills, and expertise exist to help us dig down within ourselves, search for it, and overcome them. There are so many tools available out there; use and test as many as you can. I am offering you the Octagon of Excellence Method as an excellent tool, a step-by-step guide, and a head start in overcoming whatever may be stopping you from reaching your maximum potential.

Apart from day-to-day problems like mental and physical health, emotional and relationship issues, financial and business crises, market uncertainty, rising unemployment, and customer-acquisition costs, we also face many global challenges that concern us all. Air, plastic, and water pollution, inequality, violence, global warming, poverty, racism, digital transformation, pandemics such as influenza, SARS, and COVID, ethnic cleansing, and biological warfare significant issues. Billions of us are asking, "Why do these problems occur? Is the solution really beyond human intelligence— or do we not prioritize solving them?"

Well, the answer is obvious. We have caged ourselves in an illusionary world that is full of distrust, disbelief, and misconceptions. We have been trained to think pessimistically about every problem. Unbeknownst to us, our psyches have conditioned us to give in to biased thinking. When the mind is highly polarized, it damages our physical, emotional, and mental health, and it also does the same to those who disagree with our views of the world. It drives the segregation we observe worldwide, which you can read in more detail in my multi-award-winning book, *#Loneliness: The Virus of the Modern Age.* In the book, I share powerful lessons from the twelve major life adversities that changed me forever and for the better. I also talk about the transitional stages that humanity is going through as we step into the era of digital transformation and coexisting with AI. Those who want to understand how a lack of awareness, education, and not knowing how to use the duality of our nature to achieve mindfulness will find this book very useful—and so will those who are seeking answers to solving this self-destructive global phenomenon. We form a distorted view of the world by giving in to our fake personas, which is the root cause of all evil. Instead of objectively looking within for solutions, we've learned to blame others for our predicaments.

Many of us never dare to take a stand on these issues, and those who do end up having fierce arguments to defend their points of view. Neither leads us anywhere. A barrier to independent thinking has made many of us forget how to think objectively, rationally, and out of the box. It sabotages your growth as an authentic individual, parent, teacher, friend, sibling, leader, team member, or nation. Ultimately anything is possible for the world we all inhabit and share.

To save the sanctity of human life and leave behind a better world than we found for future generations, we need to grow into our full potential. In doing so, we can take a stand on these issues collectively. It is not that difficult because the solution is already inside us. All we have to do to get those things back on track is explore our deeper selves and reconnect with our authentic and divine natures. Spiritual and material growth is just one sparkling light that will illuminate your life if you know where and when to light it without making it fade away. Don't let it remain lost somewhere within your inner self.

I love writing books that assist people in breaking through seemingly impenetrable intrinsic frontiers. I wrote this book to give you the Octagon of Excellence Method and make you surpass and conquer your inhibitions and transmute your potential into its utmost service, which is divinity.

By learning, growing, and committing to a more significant cause, I changed my entire persona—inside out—and you can change yours too. The ultimate purpose of life is to continuously commit to achieving our full potential. To fulfill as many voids as you can, strive to be in alignment with your true authentic self, have an astronomical vision, invest all you have in all you want to create, and use all you learn in the process to be of service to a more significant amount of people.

Your existence in this world is a message to upcoming generations. It is up to you to leave an inspiring legacy that positively affects their lives. Even if nobody in your surroundings is serious about solving these global issues, start with yourself. It is what I did, it is what many of the respected teachers I consulted with did, it is what all of my clients do, and it is what you can do too.

You may have a solution inside of you to turn those harmful products into more environmental-friendly goods that are great for you, the atmosphere, and the planet. Perhaps you can transform education, health care, politics, or social inequality. No matter what it is, your body, mind, heart, and soul are going to thank you for that. The more you use all you are learning to be more aligned with the universal laws that govern life, the more your intuition and manifestation abilities will increase. You will feel a drastic improvement in your overall spiritual, mental, physical, social, emotional, relationship, and financial well-being.

I have seen thousands of examples in my life—including teachers, clients, and myself—of people never giving up on their dreams despite any challenges. I don't think we have any reason to say goodbye to our callings, which come from the depth of our being, our divinity. It is wise to stay committed and focused and remind yourself that there is still a chance of victory as long as you are alive. No matter where you are, if you have enough will to do something, you will surely succeed—regardless of the obstacles.

In a seminar I attended, Dr. John Demartini said, "A master lives in the world of transformation, not the world of loss and gain." That is what Aristotle and other philosophers believed, and since I was a kid, I believed it too. When I heard John saying that, I no longer felt alone, an outcast, or a misfit, which I had been led to believe all of my life.

To step into your divine nature and reach brilliance, you need to keep creating the necessary breakthroughs to transcend to higher levels of awareness and not fall for the pain and pleasure of your animalistic nature. It would be best if you kept in mind that excessive attachment to guilt, shame, or pain is harmful to your mental health, which leads you to more of the things you do not want in the first place.

Each phase of your life demands a new you; do not fear bringing the change and embracing the challenges that come your way. It is wise to keep your movement between pain and pleasure pretty smooth to avoid the massive fluctuations in the discomfort you experience as you go through the transitional growth stages of life. The magic lies in accepting the harsh reality of life that you own nothing in this world except the love you take with you—and maybe the impact you make on other people's lives with your love, encouragement, and inspiration.

Spending our lives so that we have no regrets in the end is a meaningful way to live. This way, while taking our last breath in this world, we are relieved to know we have lived each moment to the fullest and have lives according to our hearts' desires, dreams, and callings. We never know when our time on this earth will be up, and it is up to each of us to make sure that we indulge more in the activities we love and that inspire us. Focus more on leaving fantastic lessons for children to take inspiration from your life stories. You are precious, valuable, and worthy, and you are an inspiration to many children, teens, and adults. Your feelings, emotions, words, and memories deserve all the love.

We are often too hard on ourselves, and we do not focus enough on feeling contentment. We think more about other people's opinions than our own. Today, after having spent years in personal development, I can confidently say that other people's views that trouble us do not matter in life. Focus on making each day beautiful for yourself and stop caring about what others think of you. It is just a perception, an opinion, and a description written on the sandy beach that disappears with each incoming wave. As long as you are not consciously doing things to hurt anybody in your surroundings, you are free to create the empire of your dreams. You deserve to be treated with all the affection, love, and kindness you give to other people.

Spending your life so that others take inspiration from you is a matter of making that choice. Be the best version of yourself so that you don't have any regrets in the end. Live each moment to the fullest. Continue shining in every aspect of your life and spreading the magic of positivity, humbleness, and kindness everywhere you go. Stop waiting for tomorrow. Use the Octagon of Excellence's eight-step process to make an action plan today and move toward betterment each day. Always remember that you are worthy of giving and receiving an abundance of love, wealth, and wisdom. Your words can make a significant impact on someone else's life. Do not hold back from sharing your life incidents, success stories, failures, accomplishments, lessons, and fun moments with others. You never know how much encouragement it can provide to someone to keep going in dark times.

We can add so much love, hope, and positivity into people's lives just by the power of our words. It's time to realize your actual worth, decide what excellence means for you, and tell others about the beautiful journey of your life. The world needs it! Many people out there need the hope of light, encouragement, and inspiration to follow their dreams. So, why not share your powerful words with them? It can transform billions of lives. Someday, you will be so proud of yourself for spreading the message of positivity into this chaotic world—and you will smile at your choices from wherever you end up. You will be happy to know that you are gone, but people in every corner of the world are benefitting from your precious life journey, teachings, and experiences.

I hope you enjoyed learning from this book as much as I did writing it and sharing my life journey, lessons, and experiences with you. Nobody in the world is perfect. We are all equally perfectly imperfect. We are flawed in some ways and perfect in others, but the idea is to lift each other at all times and offer a helping hand to all those people in need. For example, the skills you might possess in abundance may not be someone else's expertise—and vice versa. It is our collective responsibility to be an agent of positive change in people's lives and encourage them to live their wildest dreams.

Thank you for coming on this journey with me. I trust the following statement I shared at the beginning of our journey together: "Yes! I *am* destined for excellence—and I *can* achieve it!" I hope that rings true for you now. Let me leave you with a message worth sharing: "Keep learning, for what you master becomes what awakens others to embrace their callings, excellence, and gifts hidden in the infinity of their divinity."

With love and wisdom,
Tony Jeton Selimi

Who Can Benefit from Using *A Path to Excellence?*

Whether you are daydreaming about an ideal life, a loving relationship, a beautiful home, a dream car, a new career or industry, a big promotion, becoming an Olympian, an award-winning actor, singer, or producer, an influencer, financially independent, setting up your own company, or growing your business, *A Path to Excellence* creates a clear pathway to the future you want now.

It is for you if what you are doing today to make your dream future come real matters. I wrote it for people who want to achieve audacious goals, take significant action, and learn how to make small changes every day, think big, and act with certainty and objectivity.

If you are looking for a practical framework to keep you moving toward achieving your goals, *A Path to Excellence* will help you get out of your way and propel you down the path to growing into your potential, achieving the success you deserve, and transforming you from dreamer to doer!

This book is ideal for:

- CEOs, leaders, politicians, business owners, entrepreneurs, and start-up owners
- HR, communication, sales, marketing, and customer relations departments

- scientists, psychologists, psychiatrists, social workers, doctors, nurses, the NHS, and other health and well-being professionals and institutions
- life, business, leadership, executive and corporate coaches, mentors, financial specialists, healers, therapists, personal trainers, consultants, and even United Nations delegates and peace ambassadors
- parents, professors, teachers, children, students, educational institutions, and prison workers
- film producers, directors, actors, musicians, and artists
- anyone else who wants to learn more about turning challenges into stepping-stones, emerging as the confident leader, or achieving their highest potential, and leaving an immortal legacy

What's Next?

Instead of giving in to negative self-talk, the voices of not being good enough, the feelings of feeling frustrated, powerless, and stuck, and being disengaged and unproductive, you can choose to continue to evolve yourself into your most significant potential. It's now up to you to use all you've learned to be the creator, shaper, and master of your brilliance and destiny.

I'm overwhelmed with gratitude for developing this valid yet straightforward eight-step method, which was born out of a culmination of more than thirty years of research and studies in numerous disciplines, including mathematics, engineering, technology, biology, physics, philosophy, theology, metaphysics, leadership, building wealth, business, human behavior, and psychology.

The Octagon of Excellence is a new and robust methodology for personal, business, team, leadership, and professional transformation. It assists in upgrading one's mental faculties and harmonizing the intelligence of the body, mind, and heart to deal with any challenge, doubt, fear, limit, or stress. It helps you see and use the hidden order that exists in the eight factors of life: transition, regeneration, focus, rebirth, balance, service, unity, and infinity to your benefit.

You can use the eight principles of the Octagon of Excellence to clarify, commit, confront, correct, consult, collaborate, compliment, and celebrate the good and the bad you encounter on your journey to attaining personal, relationship, career, leadership, or business excellence. It enables you to create inside-out authentic transformations that you—as an individual, partner, parent, educator, business owner, or leader—seek.

After reading this book, you might feel inspired to keep in touch and learn more about how my custom-created training and consulting using *A Path to Excellence's* Eight Cs principles can help you grow into your full potential. Or perhaps you want to introduce the Octagon of Excellence to your organization or business and turn your leaders and teams into authentic, energized, and trustworthy individuals who Gen Z and future generations want to follow. Maybe you want to invest in a business breakthrough immersion day that identifies your pain points and helps you promote excellence as a powerful tool to grow your business and renew your teams' performance, productivity, profits, and sense of purpose.

Training your employees to reach for excellence and instill empowering behaviors can eliminate the root causes of employee disengagement, poor performance, organization-wide distrust, burnout, and stress. Promoting excellence increases your corporate team spirit, sales, productivity, and overall performance. It can help your teams be more efficient, effective in closing faster on important deals, or improve your HR team by putting in place specific excellence-driving processes that will make it easier to attract and hire inspired employees who positively transform your entire organization.

The eight confidence-, excellence-, and resilience-building principles can also be used to transform an underperforming, aging health care system, tackle management, doctors' and nurses' issues, including internal conflicts, burnout, stress, and improve overall hospital staff's mental health. How about using the Octagon of Excellence Method to turn aging educational structures into twenty-second-century learning experiences?

Each of the eight principles can assist you in facing challenges head-on and mindfully, smoothly go through various life cycles, and maximize your prime asset: you. You now have a method to help you navigate uncertainty, grow into the best version of yourself, and be the change maker who others want to follow.

It would be my honor to know you since you have taken the time to remember me. I love being of service to you, your family, your business, your institution, and your country. I love contributing to the evolution of human consciousness—virtually or tête-à-tête. I love using all that I learn and master to speak, train, and consult clients like you from all over the globe, facilitating the realization and the accomplishment of your business, personal and professional goals—provided you are ready to invest the energy, money, and time required to realize your highest vision.

Booking a breakthrough consultation can help you identify what you can do to jailbreak out of the self-imposed limits of your mind, expand your vision of excellence, and lead your life with increased confidence, more prosperous personal and interpersonal relationships, and an increase in your worth, influence, and wealth.

It gives me tremendous joy to be your coaching partner who assists you in focusing all of your mental faculties to become an outstanding authority, speaker, author, coach, performer, artist, musician, sports personality, leader, entrepreneur, corporation, parent, sibling, or influential individual. Each consultation, talk, program, or training can give you the clarity you need to turn a specific challenge into a stepping-stone and harness your abilities to turn the impossible into the possible.

Clarifying what you are inspired by establishes a healthy foundation for the excellence you seek and the purpose that nurtures your creative genius. Enjoy life's journey—not just the destination—and welcome the triumphs that inspire you and the mistakes that discourage you. Embodying this awareness is a significant part of your growth, reaching a place of appreciation, gratitude, and sincere love. As you do this, inspiration will come to you when you least expect it. Any expression of your being that goes out to others will touch their hearts and overcome the challenges that lead you to excellence.

To take this work to the next level, you can download resources, take the unfakeability test, download my app, invite me to speak at your events, attend my seminars, talks, workshops, discussions, networking, retreats, or bring them into your organization and business so we can accelerate your achievements by working with me privately.

To see what's coming up, connect with me on all social media channels or learn more about what my integrated work can do for you. Please visit https://tonyselimi.com. Remember to subscribe to my Instagram, Twitter, Facebook, and YouTube channel and sign up for my inspirational newsletter so that you can receive information that inspires you to live a meaningful life, free resources, and year-round special offers.

Finally, to help others strive for excellence in their chosen fields, please review this book so that we can evolve, grow, and transform the lives of one billion people so that they too can unleash the power of appreciation, excellence, and divinity. The best news is that you will be rewarded for taking the time to do so. Here's how:

1. Write a review of this book.
2. Post it on Amazon, iTunes, a bookstore's website, *Readers Digest*, or your website, blog, Facebook page, Instagram, Linked In, or other mediums. If you are a journalist seeking inspirational stories for your blog, TV, radio, or podcast show, get in touch so we can educate and inspire your audience—or interview me for a newspaper or magazine you may be writing for.
3. Share your review on Facebook, LinkedIn, Instagram, and Twitter, tag @TonyJSelimi @apathtoexcellence, and send a screenshot of "verified purchase" with your payment receipt to info@tonyselimi.com.
4. As a thank you, you'll receive a free MP3 meditation you can use daily to energize your body and mind and automatically

be entered into a regular monthly drawing for the chance to win a one-hour breakthrough consultation.

5. If you have a favorite idea, sentence, or principle, use it as a Tony J. Selimi quote in a tweet, social media post, book, or talk—or to ignite a desire in your heart, inspire your loved ones, your social media fans and followers, your audience, and your colleagues and leaders.

Magic happens when excellence becomes the default lens through which you observe the obstacles that life presents you. When you daily integrate the eight principles shared, you become more confident, focused, and unstoppable.

Make sure you use the eight principles as a way to face daily obstacles head-on, unleash productivity, power, and purpose in the domain of leadership, business, teamwork, and selflessly pursue your personal, relationship, social, and spiritual callings in life.

If you think pursuing a path to excellence is about transforming your life, you've missed the point. It's about helping you increase the clarity of your vision to effectively and efficiently serve humanity better by exemplifying high human potential. In doing so, you will be inspired to unleash the infinity of your divinity and leave a thousand-year legacy.

Those who commit to growing into their greatest potential get to influence life.

Good luck!

TRANSFORMATIONAL
PRODUCTS

A Path to Wisdom

Distractions prevent you from listening to the built-in alarm that your body uses to alert you when something is wrong. Ignoring the body's wisdom is the root cause of disease, faster aging, fears, business and personal failures, and many psychological disorders. Life adversities have the power to bring you out of your natural state of healthy balance and into creating lower-mind animal behaviors that prevent you from realizing your highest expression of yourself.

Judgment of self and others is the biggest killer on the planet, but what if you could go from lower-mind, reactive thinking into a divine being who is objective and proactive and transcends human traits for a higher purpose that elevates your current awareness? What would be possible for you then?

This Amazon-bestselling and multi-award-winning book is a timeless life manual that offers a road map that safely guides you through an inside-out reflective journey to find and address the root cause of the physical, mental, emotional, spiritual, financial, business, relationship, self-love, self-worthiness, and self-confidence issues that keep you out of your healthy natural state of inner balance, empowering you to activate, advance, and accelerate your human and business potential.

In a volume that won the *Top Shelf Magazine* Indie Book Award, the Book Excellence Award, a finalist award in the USA Book Contest, got more than one hundred sterling Amazon reviews, and was given readers favorite five-star seal, you'll find an ocean of wisdom waiting for you to discover it.

You will learn how to use "TJSeMethod: ALARM®" to help you acknowledge, listen, act and respond to your inner voice, which is there to guide you to take back the reins of your life and harness the healing power of unconditional love. Doing all the exercises with a childlike curiosity helps you use your innate, built-in intelligent faculties to deepen your understanding of yourself, awaken you to your true calling, and honor your spirit, greatness, and wisdom.

This proven method, which was developed during thirty years of heartfelt research, can assist you in establishing an easy path to healing and transforming every critical area of your life. Complete the exercises in the book and use the twenty-five conscious creating principles embedded in the method to learn how to:

- acknowledge and own your power, be more assertive, influential, and in control of your choices and decisions
- love the duality of your nature, heal your body, mind, and soul, and listen to your body's wisdom
- achieve higher states of awareness and intelligently use all of your faculties.
- create results and live in harmony with your authentic values and your life's purpose.
- attract abundance, opportunities, and miracles into your life

Learn, apply, and use the TJSeMethod: ALARM® twenty-five principles to empower, grow and transform all of the eight critical areas of your life: For more information, please visit https://www.amazon.co.uk/Tony-Jeton-Selimi/e/B00KXBZSX0.

A PATH TO WISDOM

How to live a **balanced**, **healthy**
and **peaceful** life

TONY JETON SELIMI

Multi-award-winning, #1 Bestselling Author and Filmmaker

#Loneliness: The Virus of the Modern Age

So connected, yet desperately we are alone, drowning in an ocean of infinite possibilities.

Meticulously researched and written, *#Loneliness: The Virus of the Modern Age* explores the damaging scientific, psychological, and spiritual impact of loneliness—a problem that has become an ironic epidemic in a world that is more interconnected than ever before.

In a world where communication is instant, where billions of people can interact at just a moment's notice, it will come as a shock to many to learn that loneliness is an epidemic more rampant and destructive than at any point in history. Almost everyone faces adversity from the isolation that causes us depression, anxiety, or diminished self-esteem.

We have become accustomed to a new way of being alone in a technological cocoon that covers up our actual pain. Our true essence is hidden behind façades that we show the world from the fear of being judged, criticized, and rejected. This brings us out of a natural state of healthy balance, is the root cause of disease, and creates the segregation experienced worldwide.

#Loneliness is a global call for people to redefine themselves in the face of life's most significant challenges. Comforting, moving, and spiritually practical, this book is a guide to help you break through

your apparent loneliness and shift you toward crowd-nurtured world peace and the next stage in our evolution.

Loneliness disintegrates your mental and physical health, infects your genome, and leads to multiple changes while painting a dark and pessimistic picture of the world around you. The most surprising thing to learn is that today's obsession with technology does nothing more than awaken the segregation, discord, and loneliness already inside us all, which further spirals our moods and our outlook.

Read this book to make you aware of that problem, create a road map that safely guides you out of your disempowered states, and empower yourself to redefine the meaning of your life so that you can overcome adversity with ease and build the happiness and prosperity you so deeply crave.

Use it to reveal how inner discord creates deceptive loneliness, which is spontaneously appearing worldwide in the form of war, racism, nationalism, xenophobia, homophobia, illness, divorce, financial crises, and so much more. It is a life manual that shows you how to extract wisdom from every adversity so that you can become a more balanced, mindful, and heart-centered individual, leader, parent, teacher, and human being.

If you let it, each page will guide you and encourage you to make the changes that your soul is craving. The principles and ideas shared will teach you how to listen to your heart in ways you didn't know were possible, amplify your awareness, and ultimately break free of the cocoon that is stopping you from seeing and embracing the beauty of this world.

It goes beyond you as individuals; it will teach you how to unite and ignite humanity's collective voice so that we can progress to the next stage of our evolution. If this is your calling, get this book from https://www.amazon.co.uk/Loneliness-Virus-Modern-Age/dp/1504343999.

A balm for the restless soul yearning for connection,
freedom, and love in the desert of emptiness.
— Foreword by Dr. John Demartini, international best-selling author

#LONELINESS

THE VIRUS OF THE MODERN AGE

TONY JETON SELIMI

Fit for Purpose Leadership #3

Burnout is a significant personal and public health problem. Burnout presents itself in many forms, but the most significant one is in the way of the overworked employee who is stretched thin by too many responsibilities, too little training, too few resources, and too little time. In fact, according to some researchers, burnout has several faces.

In its third outing, *Fit For Purpose Leadership #3*, together with fifteen high-performing leaders from around the world, shares our highest-value thinking and advice on business leadership, with a focus on health, mindset, social and relationships, meaning, purpose, best practices, and emerging trends.

I wrote a chapter on burnout after consulting for many business leaders who asked me to help them cope with this growing problem. In this chapter, you'll learn how to be aware of the triggers, varieties of exhaustion, and how different symptoms require different solutions.

With a client example, you are taken on a journey that will counteract this kind of burnout through clarifying leaders' and organizations' values, aligning those values with a clear vision, giving employees clear and realistic goals, advising what they need to meet those goals, and offering appreciation for a job well done.

By tackling burnout successfully, you can also eliminate the problem of high absenteeism, low engagement, exhaustion, stress, and mental health issues that may otherwise arise.

If you want to create an environment that allows employees to thrive and flourish, promote excellent mental health, and build a healthy organizational culture, then everything I share in this leadership-focused book will help you create a meaningful and rewarding workplace that guards you and your employees against burnout.

Grab your copy from https://www.amazon.co.uk/gp/product/B07BRXF5FZ.

Best-ranked Amazon UK and Australia
#1 *Coaching and Mentoring; #1 in Teams*
and *#3 Management & Leadership!*

FIT-FOR-PURPOSE
LEADERSHIP#3

15 inspiring business leaders
share their highest-value thinking
on best-practice leadership

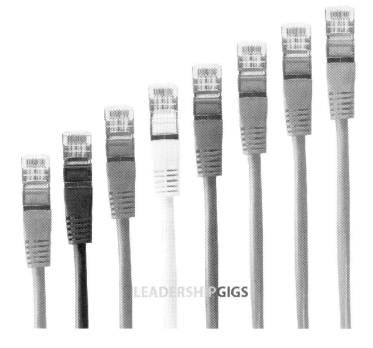

LEADERSHIPGIGS

The Unfakeable Code®

A life manual that assists you in understanding how
the law of attraction works, and it gives you valuable
insights into the science of healing and changing your
mindset that will transform your existence.
—Marie Diamond, global transformational
teacher, star of *The Secret*

Step forward a fresh new way to:

- handle judgments and rejections easily
- manage negative self-talk
- stop being a people pleaser
- use your emotions intelligently
- own your power and learn the virtue of loving prudently
- transform your scarcity persona into a thriving individual
- infuse your life with freedom
- give rise to an authentic leader who transcends the status quo
- eradicate the root cause of employee disengagement
- authentically shape your destiny and evolve your sense of purpose
- maximize your prime asset: you

This inspiring book shares some of the rules where people can
come back into authentic living, leading, and loving, where old

wounds can be healed, and masks can be unveiled. This wise-to-read book makes a compelling and scientific case for being more authentic at home, socially, and at work. It assists in effectively going through accelerated business, personal, and professional growth stages and achieving stellar outcomes. It also teaches people how to harmonize body-mind-heart intelligence in ways that help with anxiety, conflict, and stress and willfully create an inspired destiny. It helps you see the hidden order in all that life represents, defuse judgments with objectivity, and develop more grateful states of love and vitality.

The Unfakeable Code® is available in hardback, ebook, and Audible at good bookshops and online retailers. For more information, visit https://theunfakeablecode.com.

"This is an inspiring, enjoyable, fast-moving book that shows you how to unlock your full power for unlimited success." Brian Tracy, Author

THE
UNFAKEABLE
Code®

Take Back Control, Lead Authentically and Live Freely on Your Terms.

TONY JETON SELIMI

Multi-Award-Winning, #1 International Bestselling Author and Consultant

Take Off the Mask:
Your Soul is Waiting

(Channeled Poetry)

The release of a selection of Tony Jeton Selimi's channeled poetry in the anthology *Novum #10* is making waves in the world of poetry and literature. Combining more than forty years of research, studies, and inspiring testimony, the book contains Selimi's heart and soul-enriching poems and the works of other established writers, poets, and teachers.

Each of the channeled poems can unlock a chest of treasure buried inside of you and reprogram your mind with the knowledge that assists you in leading an authentic life that is filled with love, courage, inspiration, and limitless potential. Selimi's intuitive poetry is unique as each one is written for a specific person who has either challenged him to the core or has inspired him to reach for his star. The traits of these people are revealed through transcendental language in a series of poems that transforms polarized into objective thinking by waving life's challenges to its rewards.

These poems take you on a mental, emotional, and spiritual quest toward self-actualization as the author shares the lessons and the wisdom gathered from each of these individuals with words that free the mind to revel in love's delight.

This is your chance to go on a self-reflective journey that awakens you to the awareness that no mask on the outside can hide the truth your authentic, genuine, and unfakeable being knows on the inside.

Take Off the Mask: Your Soul Is Waiting is a selection of new kinds of inspired poetry that give you glimmers of hope on the horizon despite the darkness that may be lurking in every corner. Each verse hides the wisdom of how to change the way you conduct yourself and change your life. It assists in unleashing the power words carry and embodying the traits of those who challenge and support you as you embrace your unfakeable individuality. This selection of poems is ideal for those seeking to step forward a fresh new way to:

- grow mentally, emotionally, and spiritually
- look at, engage, and transform reality
- awaken the wisdom of the sages
- remove the mask of innocence, rights and wrongs, and judgment, allowing the truth about suffering's reach to come forward lovingly
- infuse your life with a limitless sense of freedom and untapped potential

Grab your copy from https://www.novum-publishing.co.uk/books/book/novum-10-1.html.

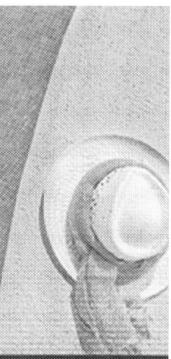

novum

#10
novum
VOLUME 6

Living My Illusion: The Truth Hurts

(Multi-Award-Winning Coaching Documentary)

In the Facebook/Instagram world, everyone thinks that Joel has made it. But when he invites a famous life coach and business coach specializing in human behavior, Tony J. Selimi, into his world, a journey of self-discovery reveals the truth, leading to a decision that will change the course of his life. A morally provoking, contextually interesting, and life-transforming true story of how a successful entrepreneur, husband, and father is willing to do what most people fear to do, but deep down, wish they could do themselves.

Through shocking truth-telling interviews and private one-on-one coaching sessions, you can see Joel's "in the moment" realizations during an original series of revealing questions by Tony, bringing him to question the realities of the life created by the masked personas he shows to the world.

Joel courageously shares deep and personal learnings, speaking honestly about using IVF to conceive a child, sexual repression, and wondering if he ever loved his wife at all. He does this without fear of any backlash. Will he succumb to his father's expectations, listen to what his friends are doing to get back in line, or follow the feeling burning inside him at the cost of hurting his loving wife?

This timely documentary about the toxic personal, family, and business effects of midlife crises and how Tony's transformational life coaching and integrated approach can help people be faithful to themselves makes a case for breaking certain taboos and adds friction from a moral standpoint.

In each snapshot of the actual coaching session, you'll see how Joel is trying to work out what the illusion of fame, fortune, and freedom means to him at the expense of his health, business, and marriage. From the other aspect, you'll learn from Tony's unique guidance, teachings, and wisdom, how you, as the viewer, can become aware of the subject's resulting actions and the midlife crisis saga that no one can escape.

Living My Illusion: The Truth Hurts, cocreated by Joel, Timea, and Tony, pushes the boundaries of the documentary form as a mirror to every persona and inviting you to reflect on the lies you tell, the truths you conceal, and the fearful and courageous decisions you make. You'll realize how questioning every societal value you uphold can help you live an authentic, inspired, and fulfilled life.

In Tony, Joel has found someone to give him the clarity he needs at a crucial point in his life, to help him find his unique voice and choose a path to living a purposeful life, giving his wife and family the greatest gift he could ever give: having Tony as their teacher to help them find their truth and ultimate freedom.

Since completion, *Living My Illusion* was declared the New York City Independent Film Festival's official opening night film and a platinum winner of the International Screen Awards, and Cardiff International Film Festival. It was a winner of the Houston International Film Festival Award, Impact DOCS Awards, Los Angeles Film Awards, Hollywood International Documentary Awards, Docs Without Borders, Barcelona International Film Festival, Amsterdam International Filmmaker Festival, Nice International Film Festival, Madrid International Film Festival, Milan International Filmmaker Festival, UK Monthly Film Festival, Oniros Film Awards Italy Finalist, and Rome Independent Prism Awards—Official Selection.

Watch *Living My Illusion* on Amazon Prime Video http://bit.ly/ LMIAmazon, leave your review, and share it with someone who is going through a midlife crisis and requires clarity.

LIVING MY ILLUSION

- A Documentary Series -
Episode 1 "The Truth Hurts"

"IT'S TIME TO TAKE OFF THE MASK"

TonySelimi.com
The See-Through Coach

vandercom

GHOST

LIVINGMYILLUSION.COM

Into Your Divinity:
Climb Greater Heights

(Documentary Series)

In a fast-paced, uncertain, and technologically advanced world, it is easy for people to lose themselves, be imprisoned by societal conditioning, toxic marriages, family commitments, memories of physical and emotional pain, doubts, and fears, and end up moving with the crowds and create their lives based on the expectations of others. This way of fearful living forces many people to do what everyone else's voices tell them what to do and forgetting their true calling in life: expressing, sharing, and loving their divine nature. Millions, if not billions, of people find themselves feeling alone and stuck in an ocean of infinite personal, professional, business, and financial chaos, trying very hard to meet the most fundamental human need: survival.

They learn to suppress their pain's voice and hearts' desires to fit in and seek approval from those they love so they can feel worthy and be accepted. Given the prevalence of the consequences and its adverse outcomes, Tony felt called to create this documentary series for those who want to learn how to examine their reality objectively, become authorities in their fields, grow their brains, and make great social contributions. This offering is for people who are ready to invest the time, money, and energy in transforming their mindset, "heart-set," and businesses so they can effectively cope with what challenges, pains, and wounds them, process it, and transform their lives by learning how to step into the authentic power of their divinity.

Each episode of *Into Your Divinity: Climb Greater Heights* series captures your life-transforming journey as you follow your heart's voice. To be considered for this once-in-a-lifetime opportunity to turn your challenges, frustrations, and pains into purposeful documentary that helps others grow and builds your authority, credibility, influence, and profile, you will first need to book an immersion day with Tony J. Selimi, the world-renowned human behavior and cognition specialist, who is known as the instigator for excellence, freedom, and growth. If accepted, you will be committing to at least one year of combo coaching and Vital Planning training. As your coaching partner, he will assist you in transforming your personal, professional, business, and financial lives and turning the lessons learned into an inspiring documentary film that can support you in building your authority, credibility, impact, and influence.

On this equally challenging and supporting journey, you will set off on an unlearning and relearning adventure of a lifetime that uncovers the root cause of your life and business struggles. In forcing yourself to venture into the unknown, you will come to realize that failed careers, businesses, marriages, relationships, and dates are not the only threats lurking beyond your current trying-to-survive path.

Some of you may doubt your abilities to create the investment needed to honor your hearts' desires and family and societal commitments. To capture your transformation in real time and experience the magic of Tony's integrated and holistic work, you will commit to investing your energy, time, and money to create results that very few do in such a short time.

To accelerate your growth, transformation, and success, you can do as many Vital Planning for Elevated Living Business and Life Mastery Programs a year as you want at a special price. You are guaranteed to walk away from this advanced learning experience with a new awareness and tools you can use to heal old wounds, get unstuck, pay off debts, give birth to new ideas, books, products, services, increase your salary, build a purposeful business, become known and successful, grow your wealth and influence, and end up being part of an inspiring and astronomical vision that grows you to your fullest potential.

Through shocking truth-telling interviews and private one-on-one training and coaching sessions, you can experience "in the moment" realizations during an original series of revealing questions by Tony, bringing you to question the realities of the life created by the masked personas and associated pains you may be showing to the world.

This opportunity is for people who want to make a greater impact, courageously share deep and personal learnings, speak honestly about their struggles, challenges, failures, fears, and successes on their journey to get what they want as well as grow their businesses and become financially independent. It is for people who desire to transform the fear of any backlash into service for others to excel. Should you succumb to the expectations of the disempowered personas you have built over the years, what your parents, partners, children, and friends are doing to get back in line, or follow the feeling burning inside of you—at the cost of hurting those you are judged and traumatized by?

This timely documentary series is about the toxic personal, family, and business effects of mental, physical, and emotional pain many people have and how Tony's transformational life and business integrated approach to coaching and mentoring can help them be courageous, faithful, and truthful to their authentic self. It makes a case for breaking certain taboos and adds friction from a moral standpoint.

In each snapshot of the actual coaching session, you'll see how your transient persona is trying to work out the illusion of various life challenges you may be going through and what freedom, success, and wealth mean to you at the expense of your health. You'll also learn—from Tony's unique guidance, teachings, and wisdom—how to become aware of the subject's resulting actions and the midlife crisis and the human predicaments saga that no one can escape.

Into Your Divinity: Dancing with Pain, Episode One created by Tony J. Selimi, pushes the boundaries of the documentary form, being a mirror to every person, inviting you to self-reflect on what pain teaches you. The lies you tell, the truths you conceal, and the fearful or courageous decisions you make can change the course of your life. You'll realize how questioning every societal value you uphold can help you live an authentic, inspired, and fulfilled life.

In Tony, many of his global clients find someone to give them the clarity they need at a crucial point in their lives, helping them find a unique voice and choose a path to living a purposeful life, giving to all they associate with the greatest gift they could ever give, and living with authentic values, truth, and freedom—with love leading the way.

Follow and watch *Into Your Divinity* once is out, leave your review, and share it with someone who is going through a personal, professional, business, relationship, career, or financial crisis and needs clarity. To be considered, please book an initial consultation by sending an e-mail to info@tonyselimi.com.

Into Your Divinity®

Dancing with pain

Climb Greater Hights
Documentary Film Series

intoyourdivinity.com

Mindfulness for Higher Productivity, Performance, and Profits

This Udemy online course is designed to help you use mindfulness for higher productivity, performance, and profits. In the study, Tony shares his transformative mindfulness principles that people worldwide use to cope better in highly pressured work environments and their daily grind. He explains how to use the TJS Evolutionary Method: ALARM® and TJS Mindfulness Pyramid, and he walks you through exercises that identify the unmet needs that cause you to underperform, procrastinate, and withdraw from life. He also shows how mindfulness can help in three critical areas of your business life:

Productivity

- dealing with a head full of noise
- identifying and defining a lack of clarity and mission purpose
- developing your vision and mission purpose
- introducing the value of planning for productive living.

Performance

- explaining negative self-talk
- demonstrating the issues around a lack of emotional mastery
- identifying the problems around entrepreneurial loneliness
- helping break the cycle of poor time management
- covering the critical mindfulness principles

Profits

- the importance of profit
- becoming a better listener
- the dangers of fear, both in terms of success and judgment
- awareness of credibility and value
- lack of communication ability
- lack of alignment

By the end of the course, Tony will have explained how to live in purpose and start on a path toward a more productive, high-performing, and prosperous life.

The course is accompanied by an inspiring twenty-eight-page workbook that is packed with practical exercises and information that is designed to maximize your investment in this course.

You'll learn the origins of mindfulness and how it can be used to help you be more productive and prosperous and perform better in any of the areas of life you choose to improve.

The TJS Mindfulness Principles can benefit you as an individual, as an employee, and the organizations you may be working with. You can use the principles to change behaviors, feel better, calm your being, make faster decisions, and more.

You will learn how to make empowering choices when the going gets tough in your life.

You will learn how to transcend the human-made cultural landscape, question the rules, and use conscious engineering processes to change your reality and so much more. The only course requirements or prerequisites are a willingness to learn and an open mind

This course is ideal for entrepreneurs, coaches, speakers, authors, and individuals who work in highly demanding roles and in environments and organizations that expect high performers and high achievers.

TJS Evolutionary Meditation Solutions

There is growing scientific research on the effects of mindfulness and meditation practices. The results are showing that they help you sleep better, feel more energized, heal faster, make more rational decisions, and change the shape of your brain.

Imagine what you could achieve if, in your mind, you had access to a *Star Trek: Enterprise* holodeck where you could play any possible simulation that instructs your subconscious mind to create a whole new reality for yourself.

This is what inspired Tony J. Selimi to create "TJS Evolutionary Meditation Solutions," a set of guided meditation exercises that help you relax, heal, get creative, get energized, get innovative, and become more alive, focused and beautiful inside and out.

Each meditation will take you on a profound inner journey to unlock your true potential. Committing to doing at least one meditation daily will help you open up multidimensional awareness and healing capacities, develop your intuition, and experience an expanded version of yourself.

Use them with *A Path to Wisdom, #Loneliness, The Unfakeable Code®,* and *A Path to Excellence* to accelerate your journey to be unfakeable with—and increase your awareness o—your relationship with all that is. You can use them at home, at work, in the park, and when you travel to unveil the true beauty that waits for you inside you.

Give yourself the gift you always wanted: the gift of stillness, self-love, and self-awareness of the divinity of your infinity. Meditating before you go to work, on your break, or before bed will help you transmute any negative energy into satin-white purity and keep your energy and vibration levels high. As you feel your inside shifting, what you attract in your life will shift. This is a joyous cocreated experience in which you'll have a lot of fun redesigning your reality.

Your mind wants you to feel good—and, deep down, you want to feel good about yourself, but your brain is busy making you feel good in other ways. No more excuses. Now you can use daily TJS Evolutionary Meditation Solutions to help you heal your body, mind, and heart, activate your inner doctor, relieve emotional and physical pain, create inner peace, energize your body, and so much more.

To download them on iTunes, use the following links:

- http://bit.ly/MeditationToBeAMoneyMagnet
- http://bit.ly/MasterYourEmotions
- http://bit.ly/BlissfulMind
- http://bit.ly/AwakenYourInnerDoctor
- http://bit.ly/AwakenYourHeart
- http://bit.ly/TransformDailyNegativity

You can also download them as an album from Tony's website. To be kept informed of when a new meditation is available, please sign up to receive his educational, inspirational, and promotional newsletter at https://tonyselimi.com.

Vital Planning for Elevated Living

Are you ready to invest five days in experiencing the ultimate personal and business growth adventure? If so, the Vital Planning for Elevated Living life-enhancing, mind-calibrating, and heart-opening symposium is a choice your future self will thank you for.

It is an exclusive opportunity to have Tony J. Selimi, one of the world's most respected teachers, a leading elite life coach, and a business mentor who specializes in human behavior all to yourself to create the breakthroughs you desire. He will help you dissolve emotional charges, answer all your questions, and teach you how to use *The Unfakeable Code*®'s five mind-upgrading codes, ten behavior-changing principles (BCP), and the twenty-five mind-conscious-engineering principles TJSeMethod: ALARM® to realize your human and spirit potential.

It is a fully customized and flexible learning experience held in beautiful locations around the world so that you can focus on what is most important to you. You can use this time to build an inspiring vision, clarify your purpose in life, give birth to original work, start, grow and expand your business, become a confident leader, speaker, successful author, or create a step-by-step plan to empower all the critical areas of your life.

This is your opportunity to transform any challenge you are currently facing by working it through with Tony. Previous clients have mentioned how quickly he got to the heart of the matter, helped them identify what was holding them back from being inspired and successful in life, and provided a resolution that turned their specific challenges into stepping-stones.

He will give you personal and powerful insights to transform undesirable situations into favorable outcomes for financial, family, emotional, leadership, health, and business challenges.

This exceptionally advanced learning experience was designed for successful, committed, and high-aiming entrepreneurs, business owners, leaders, celebrities, influencers, and other change makers who are committed to living authentic lives and being of service to others at a level few have ever had imagined.

For more information and client testimonials, please go to https://tonyselimi.com.

VITAL PLANNING FOR ELEVATED LIVING

Life Enhancing, Business
Growing and Soul Enriching
Advanced Learning Experience

CLIMB
GREATER
HEIGHTS

Tony J. Selimi
The Cognitive Expert Delivering Solutions for
the Evolution of Human Consciousness

TONYSELIMI.COM

Notes

Printed in the United States
by Baker & Taylor Publisher Services